HARD THINGS

HARD THINGS

MARC HOPKINS

atmosphere press

Published by Atmosphere Press

Cover design by Matthew Fielder

Atmospherepress.com

For my mom, who worked miracles and then worried it wasn't enough – thank you for all your sacrifices and love.

For Shana, my life is infinitely better because you are in it – thank you for being wonderful, amazing you.

BIGFOOT 200 AID STATIONS (2017)

	Aid Station	*Cumulative Distance*	*Distance to Next*	*Elevation Gain*	*Elevation Loss*
Start	Marble Mountain	0	12.2	3,280	2,743
1	Blue Lake	12.2	18.1	4,428	3,166
2	Windy Pass	30.3	9.6	1.567	1,487
3	Johnston Ridge	39.9	6.6	412	2,099
4	Coldwater Lake	46.5	18.7	5,105	3,909
5	Norway Pass	65.2	11.1	2,037	1,558
6	Elk Pass	76.3	15	2,543	3,144
7	Road 9327	91.3	11.2	2,817	2,860
8	Spencer Butte	102.5	9.6	1,282	2,852
9	Lewis River	112.1	18.9	5,472	3,315
10	Council Bluff	131	9.8	1,749	1,487
11	Chain of Lakes	140.8	17.3	3,927	3,900
12	Klickitat	158.1	19.4	4,919	4,987
13	Twin Sisters	177.5	16	2,592	4,760
14	Owen's Creek	193.5	13	385	1,639
Finish	Randle High School	206.5			

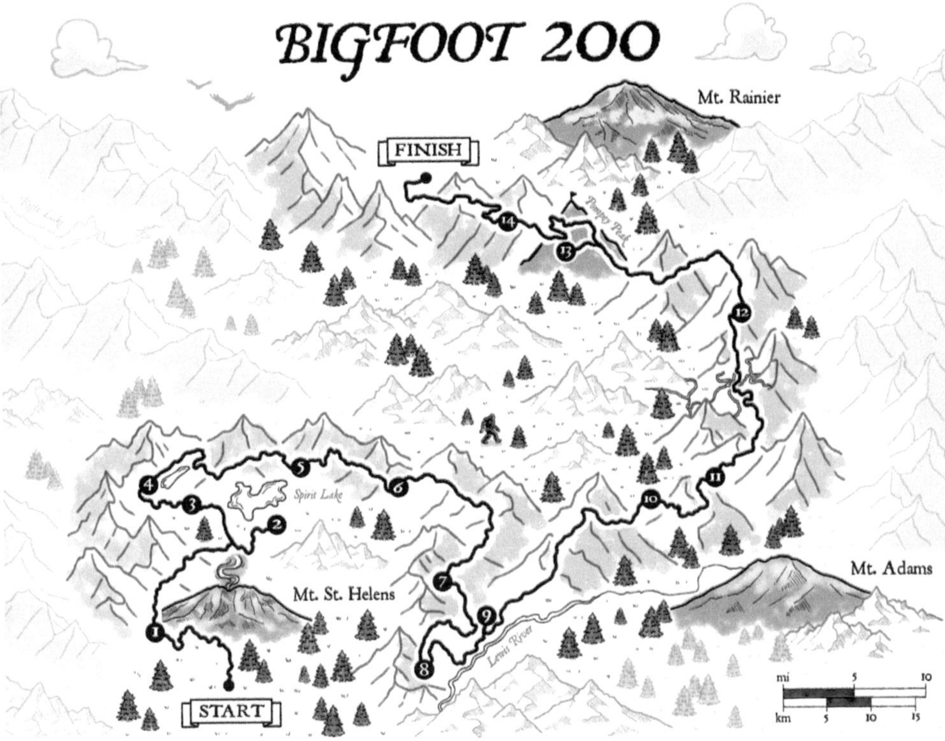

BIGFOOT 200 ELEVATION

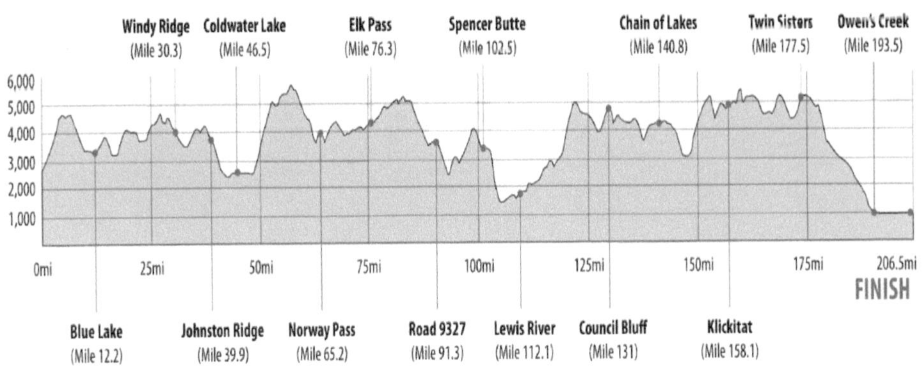

1

I moved forward slowly, counting each time my left foot touched the ground. 17... 18... 19... 20. At twenty, I stopped walking and started counting slowly to ten. Baking in the hot sun with no shade in sight, sweat covered my body.

Sweat is good, it means I'm drinking enough.

Twenty more steps up the steep incline in the intense heat. My heart rate was high, I could feel it pumping in my chest, hot blood coursing through my veins. I stopped again, breathing hard for a count of ten. Then twenty more steps up. Counting kept me from thinking about how hot it was, how much it hurt, how tired I felt. A welcome and needed distraction from this training run.

I paused again, sucking in air, surrounded by bare earth, rocks, and a few sad bushes. There was not a cloud in the sky above me, just the unfiltered sun beating down. Trees were visible well off in the distance, but there were none here to provide shade. The trail ahead continued up, but it was the only way forward, so I lumbered on. This run had degenerated into a trudge. Twenty steps, rest for ten counts, repeat. I'd been doing this for fifteen minutes without glimpsing the summit, each step a crisis, each breath a negotiation.

Why am I here?

This was, after all, voluntary—no one was chasing me. I knew the question was deeper than simply training for the brutal 200-mile footrace through the mountains that loomed in my future.

You're not even a good runner.

It was a brutal but honest thought. Yes, I ran long distances, yet the voice in my head told me I wasn't fast enough to call myself a "runner." This was just a hobby for a man with "big-boned" genetics and little athletic talent.

No one I came across on this trail would mistake me for an athlete. The last time I was under 200 pounds was in early high school. At six feet tall, I wasn't overweight, but I wasn't lean either. If someone referred to me as an athlete, people would assume I was a football player, or maybe rugby. I wasn't good or fast, yet still I ran and always finished. I was the tortoise, strong and steady, watching the hares disappear quickly. Unlike the fable, however, I never passed them, even if they dared stop for a really long nap.

In the distance, the Cascade Mountains displayed their snowcapped peaks as if to tease me as I breathed in the hot, dry air. Living in the Pacific Northwest, forty miles south of Mount Saint Helens, I'd checked the weather before this run. The forecast had been "moderate," which since morphed into "sauna."

I want a job like weather forecasters, where everything is a percentage chance, so I'm never wrong.

I would have been out here anyway. One never knew what race day would bring, so part of the training was embracing whatever punishment the Trail Gods schemed up. Weather was just another form of enduring, both my philosophy and my pathology.

Aside from reminding myself I wasn't a typical runner, I couldn't answer my own question about what I was doing here. My mind had become reduced to counting. Twenty, then ten. When that became too much, I shortened it to fifteen steps. This worked for a while as I melted, but then that became too much, so I shortened it again. Now it was ten steps up the hill, exposed to the scorching heat, rest for a count of ten, repeating like a metronome. Stopping wasn't an option.

The way out was ahead, there was nothing else.

Even in my youth, I wasn't a good runner, I found the energy to remind myself amidst the suffering. Other than playing tag, I rarely ran at all, though it was never far away. I was a young child during the American running boom of the 70s, with American Olympic marathoners Prefontaine and Shorter regularly making news headlines. People jogged for recreation, including my parents.

Swept up in the moment, they registered themselves, my brother, and me for a local 5k race when I was six years old. Everyone else wanted to run at their own pace, which left me traversing the course alone, a tiny figure in blue shorts, white tube socks with red stripes, canvas school shoes, and a yellow tank top.

My little legs kept pumping as I ran along the city streets, following the crowd. Much like today, I didn't know what I was doing out there, only that I needed to keep going to reach the end. Two miles in, I came upon a steep hill that went up for a few blocks. I put my head down and started powering on up. About halfway, I passed my older brother as he was walking, all energy spent. He never caught me. Now four decades later, I felt a brief moment of pride in this minor victory.

I pushed myself another ten steps upward and stopped for another ten-count.

The top has to come soon.

I could quit. The thought had crossed my mind several times. But quitting would only extend my suffering. If I stopped, I'd still be on this trail with the same hill to climb. My car would remain several miles away. Stopping wouldn't end the journey, it would just prolong it. I counted another ten steps.

I looked up into the blue sky, watching a vulture fly overhead.

You won't get me yet.

As I paused for another count of ten, I tried to recall when I'd next run after that childhood 5k. It must have been junior high, when I'd signed up for every after-school sport there was, regardless of my ability. I enjoyed the physical effort and the camaraderie, but very much like running, I displayed no particular talent.

When cross-country season came around, I signed up. I stayed in the middle of the pack during races, collecting participation ribbons. Our coach, Mr. Benninger, was a marathon runner, faster than all of us. One afternoon, we found ourselves at the bottom of a very large hill at the same time. We locked eyes in an unspoken challenge, and the race was on. As we powered upward, somehow I kept pace. I glanced over, and he was taking it seriously, really trying to beat me.

After being neck and neck for the first three quarters, he surrendered to a walk, gasping for air as I ran on up the hill. At the top, I had to walk for a while before I recovered enough to jog it on in. He reached the summit and got right back to his fast pace, leaving me behind.

Still, on that day, on that hill, I had won. I didn't know it then, but these two small running experiences provided a glimpse of what would become my superpower. Not speed and not grace, but the ability to continue when it seemed unreasonable.

The trail flattened. The sun still blazed, but the level trail required less exertion. I transitioned to a steady walking pace, no longer needing to stop every few steps. I was miserable, but at least now I was moving without breaks.

After cross-country in junior high, I didn't run again for a long time. In high school, I discovered a sport I was actually good at, wrestling, and pursued it exclusively, running only when the coach made us. I did not run again for a long time after graduation. Life became way too busy as I struggled to survive.

College offered little time for recreation between classes and working two jobs that barely covered expenses. At least that was true until my sophomore year, when my girlfriend became pregnant with our son. I wasn't yet twenty. We married a few weeks later, her father jokingly holding a shotgun to my back at the altar. I was pretty sure it wasn't loaded. Everyone laughed. I chuckled nervously.

We were mismatched from the beginning, but I was determined to do the "right thing." The marriage became an endurance event long before I returned to running. We were young, from very different backgrounds, and still trying to figure out who we were, let alone how to be in a relationship. A couple years after the wedding, we added another child, in part to try and fix the problems we were having in our relationship. Three years after my daughter was born, we divorced, surprising no one.

I'd always wanted to be a dad, and I loved my kids. With a five-year-old son and a three-year-old daughter, it killed me to only have them part-time. I'd envisioned parenthood would be idyllic, like the family movies I grew up watching. Instead, I found myself alone, feeling like a failure both as a father and a person. Depression descended like a dark, cold morning fog. I started smoking, gained weight, and could have taught a master class on self-destruction.

A shadow fell as these memories surfaced. I felt it physically, as if a storm cloud had formed above me. I glanced up reflexively to see only bright blue sky. Heat waves rippled the trail ahead. I quickened my pace, more to outrun my thoughts than to make progress.

I spent a good part of my early thirties miserable, drifting aimlessly through life until I stepped on a scale at age thirty-four and found myself nearing 300 pounds. My father had exceeded 450 pounds before he passed away from a heart attack in his fifties. I was barely thirty then. Looking at the scale that day, I knew if I didn't make a change, I was doomed to become him.

A light breeze caught my attention, dancing across my skin and alleviating the heat. I shifted into a fast walk. Heat was my running kryptonite, sapping energy and elevating my heart rate, making it difficult to run. This was the toughest run I'd experienced in months, partly due to the temperature but also because of the dark mental terrain I was covering. To distract myself, I looked out at the forested mountains in the distance and dreamed of cooler temperatures.

Happier thoughts. You turned it around.

And I had. Too embarrassed to join a gym or run outside where people could see me, I purchased a treadmill so I could run inside, out of sight. I had no strategy. I ran until I couldn't, walked until I could, then ran again. Each morning, I tried to run just a little more than the day before.

Two months in, I found myself on the treadmill, tucked into the corner of the garage, a fan oscillating nearby. The machine pounded with each footfall, sweat dripping onto the belt, then being whisked away. Pinned on the wall in front of me was a poster of a forest, a trail winding into the distance. Part motivation, part cruel joke. I strained for breath, refusing to stop, eyes fixed on the path ahead.

When I glanced down at the display, I nearly fell off the treadmill in excitement. Stumbling, I hit the stop button before throwing both hands up.

"Take that!" I shouted to the empty garage.

I had run a mile without stopping, my first since junior high cross country. From there, the miles increased, and the pounds came off. As I gained confidence, I ventured outside. For the first time in years, I recognized glimpses of the person I wanted to be. Still, I wouldn't call myself a runner.

I clung to the belief that "real runners" were at the front of the pack. I was merely someone who ran.

The trail transformed into a technical section with loose rocks, tight turns, and uneven surfaces. Boulders jutted up out of the dirt like the bad teeth of some buried giant. The path threaded between rocks, some six feet high, requiring my attention to avoid an accident.

I tucked my body tight to navigate a passage between two rocks barely wider than my shoulders. I relaxed my upper body as it opened up again on the other side, though I still had to watch my footing. I was going slower, slipping every few steps as loose rocks shifted under my feet. This was a short section, but it demanded complete focus.

A raven protested somewhere nearby, but I didn't risk looking up. Nature was always moving and shifting, but I'd learned that it rarely meant danger. If it did, I would be better off getting through this section and back to the easy trail where I could run fast.

For the last fifty feet, I was forced to keep my feet in a narrow line, like a sobriety test administered by the landscape. The focus required to navigate such a technical trail did not allow space for thoughts and memories, one of the reasons I often enjoyed running them. These sections offered me respite from the internal dialogue. Soon, I emerged onto a wider path.

I was glad I'd been able to turn the darker memories from earlier in my life around and focus on more positive ones. It had been a while since my mind took me to some of the harder times in my life. That had been a big problem when I started running, almost ten years ago now.

In the beginning, it hurt. My lungs ached, muscles burned, and my mind begged me to stop. During shorter distances, there was no time for thoughts to wander, it was all about pushing.

As the distances got longer, I had to find a pace my body could maintain. With a slower pace over a long distance, my mind could engage, or more often wander, stimulated by endorphins. A gentle, almost meditative state, my "runner's high."

Before I could reach that place, I first had to deal with the basement of my psyche. The time alone with my thoughts was more torturous than the running, yet the improved health and increased confidence felt too good to let go, so I kept on. Mile after mile, I sorted through self-loathing, seeking ways to befriend the monsters within. It didn't fix anything, but I learned to like me, as flawed as I was.

The landscape transformed as I entered an area ravaged by wildfire. Charred tree trunks, a few with leafless branches clinging on, stood like grave markers. Most were black and burned, rising to fifty feet tall. Fallen branches and broken tops lay scattered randomly on the ground where the elements tossed them. Where the wood hadn't burned, it had weathered to gray. The scent of ash hung faintly in the air, like a memory. The ground was interspersed with splashes of green, evidence of the slow regrowth, none taller than my knee.

There was no shade, but a breeze provided relief. I always tried to honor where I was physically. Walking when necessary, running when possible. On the steep ascent through a furnace, I'd needed to stop every few steps. Now, with cooler temperatures and flat terrain, I was able to move faster, pushed by a familiar drive forward, a sense of urgency to keep moving.

I've observed two types of runners. Those motivated by catching someone ahead, and those driven by the fear of being caught. I was the latter, running hardest when I feel I'm being chased. Even alone on remote trails, I sensed something on my heels. This chased feeling led me to longer distances and tougher courses. All in an attempt to stay one small step ahead of the anxiety.

It wasn't just while running. I felt a sense of needing to keep moving, to keep pushing forward, in all things. When things would stall out in my life, I sought new challenges. Archery, podcasting, painting, a Master's degree. To stay ahead of the anxiety that constantly chased me, I jumped immediately into another pursuit as soon as one was complete.

Glancing up, I was transfixed by the huge wall of trees ahead. I'd run this route many times, but this transition never ceased to amaze me. Like crossing an invisible border, the barren fire damage suddenly became a lush green forest. Trees towered over a hundred feet tall, bright green where the sun hit the leaves on top, a deeper green below, creating a cathedral-like roof. The trail led through a gap resembling an arched doorway, a portal to another world.

I passed the threshold into the old-growth forest beyond. Ferns dotted the ground, moss carpeted the tree trunks, and fallen giants rotted into soil. The sweet scent of decay replaced the memory of fire. It was dark, the thick green canopy above letting little light through. The temperature plummeted, and I shivered slightly from the cooler air as my body adjusted.

The sweat began to dry from my skin, leaving a thin layer of salt. I moved from a jog into a run, feeling almost normal again.

Why am I here?

The question remained unanswered.

The thought echoed through my mind. It had been insane pushing myself through the heat and up the hills to get here. Was it worth it for just a training day? I tried to convince myself it was. That I wanted to be ready for the tough conditions the challenging—to put it mildly—race would bring, yet I knew it wasn't that simple.

My feet moved much more quietly here, the soft, fertile soil absorbing my weight. As I ran through the cool forest, I reflected on another pivotal moment six years ago. I had just completed four marathons in five weeks, my most recent attempt to outrun whatever was chasing me. I was having trouble breathing and feeling heart palpitations. At first, I thought these symptoms were due to overtraining and took a week to recover. When the symptoms persisted, I gave in and drove myself to the hospital.

Emergency room waits can be long and tedious in a room full of sick people. Fortunately, when arriving with any kind of heart symptoms, there is a pass straight to the head of the line. Within minutes, I was hooked up to an EKG.

One of the first tests they ran was to check for two enzymes in my blood that become highly elevated when there is a heart attack. In my case, one was normal, the other slightly elevated. They decided to be safe and move me onto the next test. It went like that for the next two days. They would run a test, discover a slight abnormality, then run one more test out of caution. Finally, I was given a nuclear stress test, where gamma rays were injected into my body so they could track blood flow through my heart.

"If I don't get superpowers, I'm going to be pissed," I joked to the technician as she got ready to administer the test.

"Oh, you'll get superpowers," she replied, "I just can't promise they will be the kind that do anything."

"Well, that's not the kind I want!" I countered, appreciating her willingness to play along.

The test revealed a large area of my heart was not receiving blood, confirming a problem. Based on what they could see, the doctor estimated a blockage of 80% in my main artery. This artery is nicknamed the "widow maker" for its tendency to cause fatal heart attacks, even if the person is near help. I was scheduled for a coronary angiogram first thing in the morning.

"I'm going to go through a vein in your leg to your heart," the doctor explained, "where I will assess the problem.

The hope is I can fix the blockage by blowing up a tiny balloon, maybe inserting some stents to hold the vein open. It is generally safe, but there are always risks."

He continued, "If I can't fix the problem that way, I will crack open your chest and perform open-heart surgery for a bypass." He lightly tossed a stack of paperwork onto the table next to my hospital bed. "Both procedures could encounter complications leading up to and including death. Please read through these and sign the consents."

I sat in the hospital bed facing mortality, wishing the cardiologist would have put it a little softer. I pondered my life, contemplating what was important to me. My thoughts centered on my kids, now teenagers. I knew I wasn't ready to leave them. There were many more good times to be had, precious moments to be experienced, and things left to teach them. Admittedly, due to the many poor choices I'd made in my life, the best lessons I could offer my kids were what *not* to do, but there was still wisdom in that. I wrote each of them a letter, telling them how I loved them, so they would at least have that in case of the worst.

I shivered again, this time not from the cold.

It had been six years since that day, but the memory remained vivid. I felt grateful to be interrupted by the sound of water. Up ahead was a small river, which the trail would follow for the next few miles. This area looked like the motivational poster that had been hanging in my garage as the water flowed around moss-covered rocks and under fallen logs, complete with ferns and a full green forest as a backdrop. I knew the water would be refreshingly cold, though I wasn't hot enough anymore to contemplate splashing around in it.

The following morning, I lay on the operating table, conscious but sedated, as the doctor explored my heart. I could hear them talking as they worked, their tone shifting from professional detachment to concern. The cardiologist eventually announced the blockage wasn't eighty percent as they thought; it was ninety-nine percent. I spoke up, saying loudly, "Go big or go home!" not feeling they appreciated my humor, as no one replied.

They fixed it with four stents, opening everything back up. As my cardiologist, Doctor Nguyen, later said, the lifestyle change I had made to eat healthy, lose weight, and start running had saved my life, but I could have easily been one of the people who dropped dead in the middle of a race.

"It's like cleaning out a clogged drain," he said, sounding casual about my mortality. "We went in and cleared everything out, now it's up to you to keep it that way."

I committed on the spot to be even healthier. I would eat better. I would keep running. Whatever it took. I never wanted to return to that operating table.

The river turned and flowed away from the trail. In the resulting quiet, I could hear my footsteps, a small breeze blowing the leaves above, something rustling in the underbrush, an insect buzzing by my head. Otherwise, it was blissfully silent, not a sound or sign of civilization. I absorbed the fresh air, taking it all in. I loved being alone out in nature, it rejuvenated me. This was where I could let my thoughts run free and work through whatever was on my mind.

The heart procedure transformed me. I adopted a mostly vegan diet, getting mocked by friends for saying "mostly," but I wanted to be honest about making occasional exceptions. I shed more weight. I pushed myself harder, determined to maximize my extra blood flow.

I'm punishing my body for failing me.

After the heart procedure, I became acutely aware that my time on this earth was limited, and perhaps much shorter than expected. Instead of taking it easy, I went looking for longer and tougher races to run. This was my defiant gesture against death, middle finger extended. How I could prove to myself and others that I can do hard things. I wanted people to see me as strong and worthy. Inside, I felt weak and broken.

It was easy to blame these insecurities on the heart issue, but they ran deeper. Before returning to running, I had worked punishing hours, striving to prove myself professionally. Prior to that, it had been academic achievement. "Don't worry about me, I got this" was the message I was working hard to send loud and clear to the universe.

As I ran with this realization, I recognized it went back as far as I could remember. My father left my mom with eight kids shortly after my youngest sister was born. Before he left, he was rarely around, leaving my mom to do everything. After he was gone, he paid nothing in child support and very rarely visited. Being the second oldest at thirteen, I witnessed my mother's struggle to provide for us alone. No matter how bad it got, she wore a mask of strength and courage, never revealing any cracks to us kids.

We all went along with the game, pretending everything in our lives was great and never talking about hardships. Among my family, I especially embraced this. My entire life so far had been an attempt to show I was independent and doing well, that no one needed to worry about me. The need to be seen this way was one of the larger shadows chasing me.

It was more than wanting to show the world I was strong and capable, it was a game I played inside my head as well. As one of eight kids with a hard-working single mother, there wasn't any space for my emotions. It wasn't that I was shamed for crying, feeling sad, or being angry, it was just that there wasn't anyone to witness it. When my mom was present, there was always someone in the family louder or with a greater need. There wasn't a place for me to break down, so I held onto my troubles and carried on. A habit that continued to this day.

I learned to internalize, to find a way to deal with whatever was happening on my own. When I had my heart issue, I drove myself to the hospital. I never considered asking for help, I handled my own problems. I wasn't taught to be this way, no one forced this behavior. It was simply how I evolved. My mom and family were going through a lot, and I refused to be a burden. That meant I had to be strong for everyone else and take care of myself too. This demon had been chasing me for a long time. Even now, out on this run, I felt it.

When my heart condition revealed itself, I felt compelled to appear even stronger, to work harder, to prove to everyone, especially myself, that I was okay. This was when I started to lean heavily into ultraruns of fifty miles or more. I would show my heart, myself, and the world that I was just fine, thank you very much.

This was territory I rarely explored, even privately. I shook my head in an attempt to clear my mind. Processing life's challenges during runs was common, but it usually involved work stress or immediate problems, not archeological expeditions into childhood trauma.

Coming back to the world around me, I realized I'd been running on autopilot, entirely disengaged from the landscape. I didn't recognize anything. As this was a place I ran often, I should have known right where I was. The landscape changed with the seasons, but there were always landmarks I could depend on. This did not look right. I slowed to a walk, looking for something familiar. Nothing. I glanced at my watch, which tracked my distance and speed via GPS, and saw I was at fifteen miles.

I should have known when it got quiet.

The trail I was supposed to be running followed the river—it didn't go away from it. Lost in thought, I'd missed my turn. I turned around, grateful to at least be out of the sun if I had to add extra distance. It only took a few minutes before I spotted my error, a missed turn I'd passed without noticing. Turning left, I heard the familiar river. The trees thinned slightly as the landscape became more rocky. The trail would follow as the river meandered along. With the wrong turn and slowing down for the heat, I would get back later than planned, but not enough for Jenni to worry about.

Sometimes it felt strange to have Jenni as my partner. I'd been alone for a long time after the divorce, rarely even dating. As a divorced father with heart issues, I didn't feel desirable. When I went on the rare date, I lacked confidence and tried too hard to be who I thought they wanted. It was rare to make it to a second date. I didn't make a good first impression, and could imagine her telling her friends afterward, "He's a really nice guy, but..."

After dating failures, I focused on my kids. Fatherhood brought genuine joy, and I loved being involved in their games, recitals, plays, and anything else they were interested in. As they grew older, I recognized the need for something else to organize my life around. That was when I started leaning into running.

After almost a decade of being chronically, though somewhat intentionally, single, I was mostly content and resigned to my fate. When our mutual friend Beth set Jenni and I up, I figured I had little to lose. On our first date, as soon as she got in my car, she asked, "Who *are* you?"

I laughed, enjoying the direct question. Unsure how to answer, I replied, "What do you want to know?"

"Let's start with how you know Beth?" she responded.

"I'm in a running group with her on Tuesday nights," I said, as a way to angle in running with the hope of impressing her.

"I'm in her women's running group on Thursdays!" she exclaimed.

We spent the rest of the short drive talking about how awesome Beth was, as she was a truly good person with a genuine heart. Over dinner, we discussed our kids. Like me, she had two children when she was young, placing us in a similar life stage.

Laughing, we shared stories about our kids growing up. I shared the time my son first swore at four years old, with perfect timing and inflection after dropping one of his toy cars, and I knew I had to start watching my mouth around him. She told me about her daughter overflowing the bathtub playing mermaid, leaving literally inches of water on the floor with fortunately no permanent damage.

I looked into her deep green eyes as the conversation flowed effortlessly, enjoying her hearty laugh and bright smile. Long, brown, wavy hair played on her shoulders perfectly, and I wondered briefly about how much time she'd spent in front of the mirror to get it perfect for this evening, appreciating the effort. It framed her face well, and I thought she was beautiful.

Most importantly to me, it was clear she was a kind person in every action, from how she greeted people to how she offered me the last bite of our shared dessert, which I declined and insisted she enjoy. She was friendly, and everyone we encountered parted with a smile. It was hard not to like her. We quickly became a couple, her presence brought happiness I'd forgotten was possible.

Through my endurance events and in general, I was always seeking approval, looking for confirmation that I was strong and capable, that I was good enough. Jenni made me feel this way, awed by my endurance and what I had accomplished. She loved me even though I felt broken. She made me feel truly seen, it'd been a long time since that happened.

This warm thought accompanied me to a river crossing. I carefully navigated from one exposed wet rock to another. I had on trail shoes and socks that were designed to get wet, yet I always took elaborate measures trying to keep my feet dry. Even if I knew the next river crossing was guaranteed to soak my feet, I still battled to keep from stepping in the river on this one.

I found myself precariously perched on one leg as a rock wobbled beneath my foot. I fought for balance while my eyes searched for a safe haven for my other foot, currently dangling behind me out over the water. Fortunately, the rock settled enough that I was able to swing my back foot around and onto the rock I spied ahead. Another quick hop followed immediately by a jump, and I was across the river and on my way, feet still dry.

Even with Jenni as a partner, perhaps even more so because of it, I struggled to prove myself. Uncertain what might make me feel whole, I substituted endurance events. Ironman triathlons, marathons, ultraruns, and century bike rides. I constantly sought the next challenge, attempting to outpace the anxiety perpetually gaining on me. These goals gave me the illusion of control.

If I added up all my accomplishments, it was an impressive list. Yet it never felt like enough.

Then, several months before this training run, inspiration came as I was listening to the Trail Runner Nation podcast while working out at the gym. One of the hosts described completing a 200-mile race. It was crazy for me to be contemplating this distance, yet the seed took root. I wanted to know if I had what it took to finish a race that long, if I could endure to the end. The challenge beckoned me, and I couldn't ignore it.

A quick internet search revealed that the Bigfoot 200 Endurance Run was a "challenging" point-to-point race in Washington state through the Cascade Mountains. Starting at the base of Mount Saint Helens, it traversed 206.5 miles of volcanic boulder fields, blast zones, desert-like dunes, ravines requiring ropes for passage, numerous water crossings, long mountainous ridges, and old-growth forest with hundreds of fallen trees. The course included over 50,000 feet of ascent with more than 96,000 feet of total elevation change, equivalent to climbing from sea level to the summit of Mount Everest, then halfway back up. The fastest runners finished in less than sixty hours, while the back of the pack fought to cross the finish line before the 105-hour cutoff. Many who start don't finish.

This idea percolated for days until certainty crystallized, this would be my next challenge. The ultimate test of strength and endurance. Lasting confidence in my life, my health, and my relationship lay at the end of those 200 miles.

I became distracted by the bright sun suddenly pouring down on me. There was a break in the trees here where a rockslide had cleared everything for almost a hundred yards. Without trees, only loose rock scattered down the mountainside, with a few small bushes peeking between the cracks. I knew I was getting close to the end of this run, just a couple more miles to my car. I'd already forgotten about melting in the sun, going up the hill, getting lost briefly, and all the other painful moments, leaving them behind on the trail. I picked the pace up slightly, eager to finish.

As I made my way across the gently rolling trail, I recalled the biggest hurdle I had to overcome before I could sign up for the 200 miler, convincing Jenni. While I didn't need her permission, her support would significantly smooth the path forward. We did not live together and had independent lives, but my participation would affect both the quantity and quality of time we spent together.

Training was going to take over my life, which meant less time with her. After running all day in the mountains, I would be depleted. Most crucially, I wanted her to support me during the race, to lead my crew. This meant I was asking her to follow me through the mountains over several days, leapfrogging between aid stations, and catering to my needs on very little sleep.

I assumed the long training hours and the rigorous demand of supporting me would be the roadblock. Instead, when I approached her with the idea, her concern was unexpected.

"I don't understand why you have to keep doing these long races," she responded. "It's insane, and running that far isn't healthy!"

Her concern for my health must have been genuine, since this was the first time she pushed back on any event I wanted to do, no matter how crazy.

"I will be fine," I insisted. "My cardiologist says running long distances is good for me."

"Yeah, but not 200 miles!"

"People run this far all the time, and they are fine."

"It's still dangerous," she responded.

"The race isn't for nine months, plenty of time to be ready. Besides, hundreds of people have done it." I spoke calmly, trying to avoid escalating.

"I'm worried about you," she said quietly and sincerely.

That hit home. I wasn't ready to give up, but now wasn't the time to push.

"I feel strongly about doing it, and I'd really like your support. Please give it some thought, and we'll discuss more later," I said with equal sincerity.

"Okay," she agreed reluctantly.

Over the following weeks, we revisited it repeatedly. Her concerns for my health dominated our discussions while I tried to convince her it was safe using scientific articles. She countered with conflicting science.

Eventually, she conceded. "Do it if you want to, and I'll support you, but under protest. I don't think it's a good idea, but I will accept your decision and lead your crew."

This wasn't the enthusiastic endorsement I'd hoped for, but it was a compromise I could live with.

Ahead, I could see the sun reflecting off my car through the trees, where I'd parked near the trailhead.

It hadn't been that long ago when my finger trembled as it hovered over the mouse for that last click that would commit me mentally and financially to the Bigfoot 200. In a moment of either bravery or stupidity, most likely a little of both, my finger dropped, the registration processed, and I was in.

It had been exciting at first, but now, a couple months later, it felt like an enormous weight. I had committed to something vastly beyond anything I had done before, adding to the anxiety that had already been chasing me. Fear pushed me up that hill in the burning sun, and anxiety had stalked me through the forest. They taunted me, asking if I was good enough. As I started my car to head home, I was relieved to have the torturous run over.

The race was six months away. I didn't know my toughest challenge would come five weeks before the start.

2

The first sign my weekend was not going according to plan was at the very beginning, when I stopped at a ranger station. My training runs would be mostly in state parks, and I needed to check on what permits were required. I described where I planned to be running to the ranger on duty at the Gifford Pinchot National Forest visitor center so she could tell me what was needed. As I was talking, she looked at me funny.

I didn't understand until she said, "Those roads are closed due to snow, you can't get there."

"But it's July..." I feebly said, trailing off as I realized the ridiculousness of my words. It didn't matter what time of year it was, the roads were just as closed.

"There was heavier-than-usual snowfall this year, and much of it came late in the season. 'Course, you never can count on much being open in the mountains here this time of year anyway," she explained.

I had never imagined snow would be an issue in mid-summer, my first lesson in what promised to be an education. I stood there in silence, a baffled expression on my face.

"Let me see what you have there," the ranger said helpfully, nodding at the training plan I held in my hand.

As she reviewed where I intended to run, confirming many locations were still buried under impressive quantities of snow, I considered this as part of my mental training. A test of my adaptability. I would not be able to train on the sections of the Bigfoot racecourse I had planned, but with 206.5 miles of trail, there were still plenty of options.

After some collaboration with the ranger, I had two new sections to run and two sections I would keep. One new section would be the start line at Marble Mountain Sno-Park. The other was the Lewis River section, my new starting point for this weekend, just a few miles away. I got back in my car and headed out.

It was now five short weeks before the start of the race. The past seven months of training had been grueling, but I'd pushed through. The days had not been idly spent.

I'd started training immediately after signing up for the Bigfoot 200. Seven months of preparation that had somehow led me to this climate comedy. Most participants would be seeing everything for the first time on race day, but I had the opportunity to train on parts of the actual course. The plan was to drive to a trailhead, run all day, then sleep in my car each night. Experience sleep deprivation, become familiar with the toughest sections, run on tired legs, test my nutrition strategy, and build mental fortitude. As a bonus, I would gain perspective on how these mountains could crush a runner's spirit.

July Fourth falling on a Tuesday meant I had four days to work with. By sneaking out of work early the Friday before, I would gain another half day. With Jenni out of the country on a two-week trip with her girlfriends, this was perfect timing. Though I'd had to make changes, I was still hoping to cover twenty miles this Friday afternoon. After sleeping in my car tonight, I would wake Saturday and drive to another character-building section for ten-plus hours, then repeat on Sunday and Monday. This left Tuesday to relax and recover.

Fortunately, I worked from home, an outside sales job I had landed several years before. As long as the sales came in and the job was done, there was freedom in my schedule, allowing me to start early some days so I could cut out early for training. Even better, on long holiday weekends such as this, my clients disappeared. No one wanted to talk to me on a Monday before Independence Day. I could easily skip out, and it made no difference.

I pulled into the parking lot for the Lewis River trailhead, found an open campsite, and pulled into the spot. After paying for the night, I dug through the back of my Jeep, around the sleeping bag, pillow, duffel bag, water jugs, and ice chest, until I located my bandana. The change in plans meant running where there was less shade. I wanted the bandana as protection, having learned from painful experience that sunburned necks and hydration packs that rub against them are a particularly unpleasant combination.

I tucked it into a pocket on a hydration pack already bulging with the gear required for race day. In the back pouch was a lightweight jacket, a headlamp and flashlight with extra batteries, first aid kit, rain gear, emergency space blanket, and a water filter. In the front pockets, easily accessed while I was running, I carried nutrition, the bandana, a pair of gloves, and my phone. There were also one hundred ounces of water in a bladder with a drinking tube and another twenty ounces of electrolyte drink in a bottle tucked into a front pouch.

The race director required everyone to use a GPS app that had the racecourse plotted on a digital topographic map, which was very useful given most of the course existed in areas where phones died of loneliness. It took several minutes comparing what was on my little screen to the landscape before I could locate the trailhead, which had been doing a good job with the camouflage.

I started slow, letting my body warm up. The trail followed the mostly empty campground before veering off into the woods. It was a well-traveled single-track, just wide enough for one. If someone came the other way, we would get to perform the awkward trail waltz. I didn't know enough to identify the trees, though they had large green leaves and were not the fir trees I had expected. They provided a cool, shady cover while allowing enough light for abundant undergrowth. Off in the distance, I could hear river music, lending a profound tranquility to the scene. I felt good, alone with nature, steadily jogging along the trail.

As I loosened up, my body eased into my normal pace, and I felt optimistic. The forest sounds, footsteps on gravel, occasional bird calls, and wind through trees composed a soundtrack far superior to my gym playlists. Having successfully adapted to plan B, I felt confident, embracing flexibility as a crucial skill for any endurance event, especially one lasting several days.

The first mile passed pleasantly before the journey started going downhill, though, more accurately, it started going up. Very up. Launching skyward as if attempting to achieve escape velocity. I started huffing and grasping at the trail with my hands.

I'm in good shape, it shouldn't be hitting this hard.

Panting, I kept going, there were many miles to cover today. The early confidence evaporated as quickly as my energy. Climbing the hill, I considered the past several months of training. 200-mile runs weren't exactly mainstream and there wasn't much information on proper training. But a 10k or a marathon? No problem finding thousands of guides. There were only two plans I could find with my internet sleuthing for 200-mile races, both hardcore, not for a turtle like me who only dreamed of finishing.

With nothing to guide me, I developed my own strategy. Weekdays meant long hours at the gym switching between bike, elliptical, treadmill, rowing machine, swimming, and climbing stairs in a futile effort to prevent monotony.

Weekends, I ran trails for eight to ten hours each day, basically running the majority of my waking hours. Saturday was for hills and technical terrain. Sunday, well-groomed trails for maximum distance, getting my body used to running on tired legs. I knew many local trails with the familiarity of a codependent relationship. It was monotonous at times, but I considered that part of building mental toughness.

According to the experts, I should have spent time on strength training to make me faster, more efficient, and prevent injury. I didn't know what exercises to do for this, and rather than research, I went with what had worked for me in the past, lots and lots of cardio. Take that, science!

Blessed rest came on Thursdays, though it never seemed enough. Coming into this weekend, I felt worn down, hoping it was normal training fatigue, even though it weighed on me more than usual.

I came upon a wide river several feet deep, rushing with the enthusiasm of snow melt. The trail appeared to continue straight into the river, with the rushing water looking too unsafe to wade through. If I crossed, I'd be up to my thighs and probably slip on a rock, making the rest of the run a soaking, miserable trudge. That is, if I didn't get hurt, left crawling back to my car while avoiding becoming some wild animal's meal. I walked up and down the riverbank, looking for an easy way across.

With no better option, I worked my way slowly to the other side by crawling and climbing from one fallen tree to another. The jumble didn't provide a direct path, so I picked my way randomly across like I was playing the world's most precarious game of Twister. After reaching the other side, I paced the riverbank up and down with dogged optimism.

Where is the trail?

Frustration arrived right on schedule. It should be here, but there was no evidence a trail ever existed. Assuming I must have entered an alternate reality, I made my way back across the scattered logs. Searching revealed only the trail I'd arrived on. So I went back across the logs to discover there was still no trail on the other side. I crossed back and forth, going a little further each time, trying to figure out what I was missing.

What is happening?

It seemed as if the trail decided to go on an impromptu rafting trip before reaching the other side. Irritation grew as I burned precious daylight hours with this idiotic quest.

Where is the damn trail!

Then, during what felt like my hundredth riverbank reconnaissance mission, I stumbled upon it. It was faint, worn away by winter, looking more like a casual suggestion than an actual path. Most people staying at the campground probably stopped at the river crossing. Any who braved crossing likely gave up on the hidden-trail treasure hunt and retreated. I was stubborn and determined, refusing to admit defeat when there was a perfectly good way to extend suffering. Candice, the race director, had promised "remote," and she was already delivering trails so rarely traveled they were not maintained.

The trail led upward, like a squirrel's tiny tracing through overgrown brush. Jogging slowly, I realized my breathing was heavier than it should have been. Still, I refused to slow down. I couldn't release the need to appear strong, even when there was no one around. Anxiety was breathing at my shoulder again, pushing me forward while doubt and fear hitched a ride on my back.

I had fooled myself into thinking I was something of an endurance expert, but the truth was that I merely endured. Endurance contained meaning and direction. It was moving toward something with purpose, a goal in mind. It was hanging in there through long, hard times to achieve a purpose.

Instead of working toward anything, I was merely surviving. I rarely felt much sense or purpose beyond trying to get past the suffering in the moment. I was simply hanging on for as long as I could, being taken wherever I was led. Over time,

I found a way to settle for whatever was happening, for wherever I was in life. Not wanting anything more than to make it through the day.

Over the next few miles, the rarely traveled trail vanished entirely, erased by winter's heavy hand, and still I pushed onward. After a bit of up and down, there was a long climb where I huffed and puffed, followed by a refreshing descent that led to another river crossing. No fallen trees this time, just a straightforward wade across freezing water.

Fortunately, the trail was easy to spot on the other side. As I kept stubbornly moving forward, I was starting to see a pattern: up, down, river, repeat. Mother Nature's tedious obstacle course.

After the fourth river crossing, the grade became steep and the dirt transformed into something like sand. Each attempted step upward was followed by my foot sliding backward, seeking stable ground. Progress required an absurd amount of effort for minimal gain.

Within just a few steps, I was cursing whoever decided this was a good place for a trail. Dusty soil turned instantly into mud on contact with my soaked shoes, while my feet started sliding around inside. Hotspots were blooming into blisters like wildflowers in spring. I kept stepping up then sliding down in a Sisyphean effort.

Through some miracle of origami, my left shoe insert folded underneath itself, leaving the arch of my foot to chafe along the thick surface of the fold while my toes hung over and bumped against the bare rubber bottom.

How did that even happen?

The ascent was unending and unforgiving. I was breathing even heavier, forcing me to slow down, but I wasn't going to stop.

This is not how this day was supposed to go.

Despite the struggle, my thoughts wandered to how, as my training distances increased, my life shrunk. When I wasn't working, I was training, eating, or resting. Everything else became expendable.

Jenni remained patient and supportive. Our relationship had never required constant contact, we could go days or sometimes weeks between seeing each other due to schedules and life, even before the training started. I tried aligning recovery weeks, when I trained less, with our plans, carving out hours, or cutting out of work early, when possible, to be with her. Still, we saw less of each other overall.

In the beginning, I had felt accepted by her for who I was. Now it seemed her approval was a carrot dangling in front of me. The less I received, the more I craved it. This dynamic displayed in subtle ways, like when I made a wine recommendation.

"Hey, you have to try this," I'd said proudly a few months ago. "It's very good yet really inexpensive. Less than ten dollars a bottle, but you'd never know."

"What's it called again?" she asked as she pulled out her phone.

"Two Vines," I answered.

She spent the next few minutes researching online before admitting, almost reluctantly, "Wow, it actually has good reviews."

While I was secretly pleased that strangers on the internet agreed with my assessment, her increasing need to validate my opinion was driving me to stop sharing my opinions.

My foot slid dramatically in the soft, unstable earth. My leg ended up underneath, then behind me, propelling me forward. I barely caught myself from a complete face-plant. Standing up, I surveyed my shoes, caked with mud. Looking ahead, I could see nothing but soft dirt continuing into the distance above. It was a miserable slog, but I was more stubborn than this mountain.

You didn't just stop sharing opinions, you stopped asking for what you want.

It was a dark truth and a welcome distraction from the physical suffering. Yet another place in my life I endured, refusing to quit. I had stopped asking because my desires felt unimportant.

I always preferred to sit with my back to a wall, so no one could sit behind me. A teenage paranoia after being teased about neck acne had established the habit, which persisted long after my skin cleared.

Early in our relationship, I didn't recall where I sat being an issue, however, a year ago, I noticed she always sat with her back to the wall. One day, I gathered the courage to speak up.

"Do you mind if I sit there?" I asked, indicating the wall seat that she was clearly angling for.

"Why?" she challenged.

"I prefer it, and I haven't had that seat for a while."

"I'd like this seat," she said and sat down with finality, leaving me to take the exposed chair.

She opened her menu with no explanation. I had never told her about the lingering discomfort from my acne. If she had an equally compelling reason, we hadn't discussed it. Neither had the simple curiosity to ask why the other preferred that seat. Instead, it continued to be rare for me to get the wall chair, and I silently held onto resentment. Maybe we both did.

Moments like this taught me not to ask for what I wanted. It felt horrible when requests were ignored. On the occasions I did receive what I requested, it often felt worse than being denied, like a charitable gift that needed to be earned rather than offered in partnership.

In contrast, Jenni knew what she wanted and went for it, admittedly steamrolling what was in her way if necessary.

Never wanting to be a problem growing up, I ended up being the pavement she rolled over.

All of this had happened slowly, like the proverbial frog boiling in water. She didn't think twice about getting her way, and I believe she assumed others did the same. Instead, I tried to support her in everything, aid her in achieving what she wanted. I hoped she would see my unconditional support, recognize how good it felt, and then reciprocate.

Instead, over time, she got more things her way, while I got less. I felt I had to work harder to earn her approval, which led to an exhausting cycle of seeking, finding, losing, then starting over. I wouldn't admit it, but part of my need to do the Bigfoot 200 race was to impress her.

It's not all bad!

I tried to avoid the self-pity spiral, reminding myself that things were great compared to my past relationships. I felt lucky she chose me. She had even been talking about wanting to move in together. Yet these distressing patterns gave me pause.

Could I be happy if this was the rest of my life?

I grunted aloud, partly to clear these thoughts and partly to defy the trail's relentlessness. Three hours in, not even eight miles covered. Laughably less than the twelve miles I'd hoped to complete by now. I was moving so much slower than I had intended, breathing heavy, and sweating profusely. I was drinking more than planned, and my water supply was dwindling.

I wasn't sure how much farther it was to the top, but it seemed like forever. I wanted to keep going, at least get to mile nine, but that was risky. Time, water, and daylight were all running out.

I turned around, defeat more painful than thirst. It was the right thing to do, but it felt like surrender. The descent wasn't any easier and I slid even more, almost falling several times.

The relationship doubts combined with the trail aggravations to deliver a punishing evening.

I knew from experience that mental preparation mattered as much, if not more than physical. The mind quits long before the body. During the race, it was not a matter of "if" but "when" I would hit a dark patch. I'd encounter the equivalent of the ten tasks of Hercules, and I knew I had to have steel determination to overcome. Countless times, I've seen people in much better physical shape drop out of races while I kept going, solely because I was in a better headspace.

I had finally gotten out of the soft dirt and onto firmer trail, but there were still several miles left to go. I kept checking my GPS watch, feeling further and further behind. I tried to run faster to make up time, but this pushed my heart rate up, so I struggled even more. The insole in my left shoe remained uncomfortably folded in half.

Friends called it masculine stubbornness. Ex-girlfriends blamed my emotional repression. But this wasn't testosterone, it was family tradition. We didn't acknowledge the existence of bad or difficult things.

I was certain that I had passed this on to my kids, just as my mother had passed it on to me. I'd wanted so much to give them a better life than I had, but I didn't have the knowledge or the tools as a young dad.

After my divorce, I refused to show any sign of weakness. I never let them see me feel sad. Never showed stress over finances. No anger. No fear. Instead, I joked and laughed, played everything down, and made it seem as if life was perfect. Just like my mother, I struggled with depression and anxiety and hid it because I didn't want my kids to worry.

I had great, loving relationships with both of my kids, yet I could never be completely vulnerable and honest. I modeled the behavior I learned, to be strong and not need help, to manage my problems alone. I could see it in them sometimes too, knowing it kept us from being closer. I didn't talk about that either.

Glancing at my watch again, breathing harder than warranted, feet feeling uncomfortable, I started to wonder if I would reach my car before dark. I was running faster than I should, this was not a pace I could maintain, but anxiety left me unable to slow down.

An uncanny childhood memory surfaced of my mom's refrigerator magnet, one of many in a large collection. It had a light brown background with dark brown writing, proclaiming "You are not stopped by the mountain in your path, but by the rock in your shoe." There was a small drawing of a shoe turned over, shaking small pebbles out. It had always stuck out to me, but only now did it occur to me.

Did I misunderstand the meaning all these years?

Considering my family's need to put on a strong front, I always assumed it meant that I should power through discomfort. Never let something small stop me.

That's stupid. Why wouldn't you stop and deal with the problem?

I had made it about powering through the hard moments, the "rocks" in my shoe, not letting them stop me on my way to the top of the mountain.

This made sense in the world of inspirational refrigerator magnets. I shouldn't let fears, self-doubt, or limiting beliefs stop me. In the real world I was living in at this moment, I was a fool for not dealing with the folded insole in my shoe. Rather, I let it fester and grow until I was dealing with extreme discomfort. Both the literal and figurative problem were better served if I would slow down and address things while they were still insignificant. Yet I kept right on running no matter how bad it got.

I knew I should stop, but it wasn't the shoe issue I was afraid of. I was scared of bigger things, like the starting line and taking on such a big challenge as this race. I questioned if I was good enough to even *be* in the race. I worried that anything short of completing the full 200 miles would prove me a fraud.

I was scared of more than the race. I was afraid of my heart problems and dying. Or of living and being unworthy. Of Jenni seeing the real me and leaving. I feared that stopping, even for a single breath, would let everything catch up to me. So, I pushed harder, driven by the need to be worthy and the fear I wasn't.

The sky had turned to dusk. I heard the last river crossing before I glimpsed it, realizing that in my mania of dark thoughts, I'd managed to run the remaining miles lost in oblivion.

I disregarded the fallen logs, this time I plunged right into the water. My feet were wet from previous crossings, and I no longer cared if I slipped and fell. The dark parts of me wished I would. As the current passed my knees, I realized how thirsty I was. I'd depleted my water supply a few miles ago, so I dipped my water bottle into the cold, rushing water and watched it fill up. It could be contaminated, but I was beyond caring and not thinking clearly, otherwise I would have remembered the filter I was carrying for this very reason.

It tasted clean and refreshing. Once the bottle was emptied, I filled it again, checking the time. I would make it to the car just before dark. A small win, but no matter how I looked at it, I couldn't consider today a success. When I woke up this morning, I believed my training was on track, and I would be ready for the race. Based on today's performance, I wondered if I could make it through the first day. My pace was too slow, I was out of breath, and I was collapsing mentally. I was facing the possibility I wasn't good enough to start, let alone finish. Unworthy of the race. And myself.

These taunts from my demons motivated me to finish strong, trying to make up for lost time. I needed to find a little confidence somewhere. This was, after all, only day one of four. It was foolish to think I could take on something this big and not have to adjust the plan, hit low points, or overcome at least one large obstacle. This day had not been a win, but neither was it game over.

I got back to my car, dumped out the river water, refilled the bottle, and devoured a cold burrito with exhausted relish. With thirst and hunger covered, I untied my shoe and pulled it off, digging inside to pull the insole back into position.

As I relaxed, the anxiety lifted. On this side of the run, it became clear why my day had been so challenging. A heavier hydration pack with all the gear. Starting too fast. Navigating unmarked, crappy trails. High altitude I wasn't used to. Spring runoff deluging the rivers.

This wasn't a list of excuses, they were legitimate reasons why I struggled. The whole run, I had been comparing my experience against my vision of the perfect training day, and that never holds up. In the moment, all I had seen was failure when I should have offered myself grace. I climbed into the back of the Jeep, curled up in the sleeping bag, and tried to get some sleep. Morning held a new trail and a new start.

It couldn't be worse than today, could it?

3

As light began to seep over the horizon, promising sun, I rolled over for what felt like the thousandth time. At six feet tall, the back of a Jeep offers surprisingly few sleeping configurations, even with the seats down, and none of them spacious. I craved a full stretch, with the night's cold adding to my discomfort. My thin sleeping bag provided just enough warmth to keep me from freezing. Last night's burrito wasn't enough food, I was famished.

As if all this wasn't enough, I had brilliantly decided it would be good training to sleep in my running clothes, including shoes and socks. I wouldn't be changing during the race, might as well get used to it now. My damp feet were protesting.

Still, I wasn't allowing myself any excuses. The race would be hard, the training should be hard. I would train for misery by embracing it. I dragged myself to the front seat, started the engine, and poured almond milk into the plastic baggie of dry oatmeal and peanut butter I'd brought for breakfast. A sense of satisfaction arose, showing my mind and body who was boss. There was a twisted happiness in the misery, exactly why I was here.

After squishing the mixture around then letting it sit for ten minutes, I had a semi-liquid meal. I tore the corner and squeezed it into my mouth. Filling carbs and peanut butter full of protein in a leak-proof package. It required no refrigeration and was an efficient way to get my nutrition, though had anyone seen they might have questioned my sanity.

I pulled out of the campground as sunrise painted the mountains, heading to Marble Mountain Sno-Park near Mount Saint Helens, the notorious volcano that had erupted with great force a short thirty-seven years prior. The trail here that circumnavigated the volcano had not been in the original plan, but was a good alternative offered by the park ranger due to the snow. It was the start line of the race, the roads were open, and it was on the way to the trail I would be running on day three. Today's plan was to go out for six hours, then turn around and head back to the car, for a total of twelve hours.

I pulled in after about ninety minutes of driving and quickly learned that "Sno-Park" meant nothing more than a large parking lot with an outhouse-style bathroom. I had envisioned a resort, or at least a large recreational area. This wouldn't be the last time my naivety caught up with me.

I should have noticed everyone else was carrying skis and wearing winter jackets as they headed out onto the trail, but I was blinded by my determination to make up for yesterday. Wearing only shorts and a shirt, I strapped on my hydration pack and jogged to the trailhead.

The first few miles were tough as I ascended, but I was feeling good. The forest was lush and green here, with several small lupine flowers blooming purple for a splash of color.

This is going to be a better day.

I could feel it in the perfectly crisp morning air. Then I hit the snow. In early July, prime summertime.

The first patch was a few inches deep and thirty feet long, the trail continuing just beyond. I crossed cautiously, confidence boosted. Then came more patches, each longer and deeper than the last. Before long, the snowpacks became so large it was impossible to tell where the trail was. I would best-guess the navigation, then bushwhack on the other side to relocate the path.

My confidence built a little with each success. I had managed the last one, so I could get across this one too. It was like going off the high dive when I was taking swim lessons. Had I been asked to jump off the tallest one right away, I would have been too afraid. Instead, the instructors had us jump off the little one that was only a few feet high. Then one a few feet higher, and so on until I jumped from the tallest diving board.

As the snowpacks built in size, I failed to notice this escalation by small increments was leading me into genuinely dangerous territory. This felt eerily familiar, it wasn't the first time I'd allowed things to slowly devolve into bad situations. If I was honest, this was happening in my relationship too. We had started wonderfully as a great couple, yet the undercurrent of critique eroded my confidence, snowbank by snowbank.

"You used too many clamps," she'd pronounced one day, examining my woodwork project, despite never having held a plane or saw.

"It is a lot of clamps," I noted with a laugh. "In order to have a strong bond, there needs to be consistent pressure along the entire glued edges, which requires more clamps than you'd think. Admittedly, like many woodworkers, I probably have a few more clamps than I need. It's a running joke among us and has inspired many a meme. Still, better safe than sorry!"

Jenni paused, continuing to stare at the glued boards. "I still think it's way too many clamps," she said factually, then walked away.

I tried to look at it from her perspective. She likely believed this was healthy criticism, just trying to help me be a better person, but each time she passed judgment, it was a small cut. With enough time, the Colorado River created the Grand Canyon, and these moments were similarly eroding my confidence.

I approached yet another snowbank. It was becoming increasingly difficult to find the trail each time. I had to choose up or down to search, and it felt like more often than not, I chose the wrong direction. Even worse, I would give up on one direction and go the other, only to realize my first choice had been right and have to turn around yet again. This meant a lot of extra up and down, and time burned. It was slow, cold, tough going.

Eventually, I was traveling almost exclusively on snow. I would reference the GPS to stay on course, but it was confusing, and several times it had me in the wrong place. If I had to retrace my path too many times, I couldn't tell which set of footprints were exiting or entering as I blundered back and forth.

The snow deepened from inches to feet. I was wearing trail shoes, but the extra traction was designed for rocky terrain, not snow and ice. I was slipping and sliding, but so far managed to remain upright.

As it got deeper, what I thought was solid snow would suddenly collapse underneath me, leaving one leg hip-deep in a hole while the other leg awkwardly remained above. A not-so-fun pastime known as "post-holing," I later learned. Each time this happened, I would pull myself up carefully before continuing miserably forward, afraid one of these times I would find my entire body suddenly under snow.

Wearing shorts, my bare legs were beat up from the rocks, tree limbs, and other debris hidden under the snow. I had hundreds of small scratches, many bleeding, up and down both legs. The melting snow joined the blood, running down into my socks.

I had gone numb, physically and mentally. It happened often when I was in tough situations like this. Like yesterday with my stupid shoe. When things got rough, I had a tendency to shut everything down that wasn't moving me forward, allowing only stubbornness to prevail.

When the going gets tough, the tough get going.

Another classic childhood proverb I'd adopted as a personal credo. When faced with difficulty, I tripled down and went even harder. Quitting never crossed my mind, nor did the fact that there was a limit to this wisdom. In certain situations, only the foolish kept going.

I plowed up icy slopes, delicately traversing angled snowpacks where a single slip would send me sliding several hundred feet down the mountain. Constantly lost, I continued trying to use the GPS app to follow a trail that had been buried for months. Fallen trees and large rocks barred the way. Progress slowed to a painful crawl, the thin air at altitude draining my energy reserves.

I had gone beyond stupid and into dangerous. I knew better, this wasn't safe, yet I had a training plan and pace expectations locked in my head that I had to accomplish. I'd invested too much and come too far to quit now. Personal humiliation from admitting defeat to all those who believed in me weighed on me. What Jenni might say when she found out worried me. The fear of failing drove me relentlessly forward.

Again, I was using more water than expected, and supplies were already running low. More concerning, the battery on my phone was dropping fast. The GPS app, my only link to the trail, would abandon me.

A little baby thought of quitting was just forming in the back of my mind when I emerged from the trees and snow to find miles of rocks varying in size from golf balls to sedans, strewn across the landscape as if dumped from above. This otherworldly landscape offered easier navigation because the Forest Service had installed tall wooden poles every hundred yards. This lunar terrain brought its own challenges as each step required testing for stability before committing my weight. Like uneven stairs, it continued for two miles before the boulders gave way to trees.

With the return of the forest canopy came more snow. The temperature dropped, and the cold started finally seeping in. The GPS bounced around erratically. The trail had vanished. After about thirty minutes of fruitless searching, I stood staring into space, taking inventory. Water supply was low, with only about a third left. Phone battery was under forty percent. GPS wasn't working. I couldn't find the trail. My watch reported five hours had passed, and I'd traveled, at best, a third of my intended distance. Once again, far behind the pace required to finish the race. Shivering in the forty-seven degree air, I realized I had yet again been defeated.

I stood motionless, searching for ever-elusive acceptance. Some kind of hope. There was only silence. I hung my head and retreated back across the lava field.

The return proved a little easier because I could follow my solitary footprints downhill, except for the areas I'd trod in every direction seeking the path. Yet the energy that had propelled me forward was gone. I moved quietly and carefully, a prisoner condemned to his fate. Like so many before me, I'd had to deal with crushing failure before as a young child trying to fit in at school, as a teen rejected by girls, and as a divorcé and single dad. Always, I found a way to swallow it down, pick myself up, and keep running. This time felt different.

Blood trickled from fresh cuts as snow continued collapsing beneath me, even in places it had held up before, yet I was struggling with my mind more than the terrain. I tried to look realistically at the facts. Hills made me breathe heavily. The terrain here had worn my legs out far faster than any other training run. My pace was far too slow to finish, not counting additional time for eating and sleeping. My body was bruised and bleeding, muscles aching from exhaustion.

I didn't believe I could complete a 200-mile run. It was doubtful I could complete a hundred-mile run. Even fifty seemed daunting. The next two days of training promised tougher trails on tired legs. No matter how I did the math, no equation equaled me finishing the race.

Attempting another trail tomorrow would mean another demoralizing day, but going home meant quitting. Not just this training weekend, if I stopped now, I quit everything. The race would be over for me before it even began.

I didn't want to surrender. My worth depended on my strength. I was the guy who could endure anything. For eight months, I'd centered my identity on this event. Who was I if I couldn't do it? What would people think of me? I imagined the words that might come out of Jenni's mouth, "I knew you couldn't do it."

This wasn't something I could power through. The boundary of my endurance had been discovered. I knew when I got back to my car, I was going home.

It was over. The training. The race. Everything. It was all over.

I continued my death march, urgency gone. Admitting I wasn't ready for the Bigfoot 200 felt like a catastrophic failure, but deep down I knew I'd built that reality myself. My life had been a series of navigating unstable snowbanks. I'd let my worth depend on increasingly unrealistic expectations.

I was glad that Jenni was out of town. I would have to tell her eventually, but to come back to her in defeat today would have been too much. I would tell her next week when she got home. Until then, I would try to process the failure.

No true friend would judge me for making the call, but that didn't matter. I was only listening to the judge in my head.

Returning to the trailhead, I remembered the morning's optimism and had a brief moment of hope. What if I wasn't a failure? What if I was good enough just as I was?

The thought dissipated quickly as I reached my car. I took off my pack, loaded everything in, and drove home broken and defeated.

4

I pulled into my driveway as the sun was going down on a quiet, cloud-covered night. Without thought, I grabbed the cooler of food and left everything else in the car, a decision that would later force me into an awkward reunion with my abandoned gear, like meeting an ex at a coffee shop. After she hadn't showered for a month.

My movements lacked energy and emotion as I unloaded the contents of the cooler into the fridge, each item a small monument to optimism betrayed.

Peeling off my clothes as I shuffled down the hall, I tossed them into a pile on the bathroom floor, unusual for me. I generally aimed for the hamper just a few feet away with the accuracy of a second-string Junior Varsity player. But even this limited precision, like my race plans, had apparently abandoned me. After starting the shower to warm up, I brushed my teeth while studiously avoiding my reflection. I didn't think I'd like what I saw.

Standing in the shower, I watched the grime from my body flowing off and down the drain. The blood from the hundreds of cuts on my legs swirled with the muddy water against the white ceramic like an art piece called "Surrender, Mixed Media."

I felt nothing.

I usually loved this, the reminder of all the hard work out on the trails. Not today. It felt more like a trope in a low-budget TV show I was watching, detached and half asleep on the couch. After cleaning up, I stepped out of the shower, threw on comfortable pajamas, and collapsed into bed like a felled tree whose roots finally gave out.

When I woke up the next morning, there was no compelling reason to get out of bed. Jenni was halfway across the world on her trip, blissfully enjoying her vacation. Friends and family would assume I was still conquering the wilderness because I hadn't told anyone I'd surrendered. I rolled over and went back to sleep. The second time I awoke, I picked up a fantasy novel Jenni had gifted me and started reading. Dragons and wizards seemed more manageable than real life and kept me from dwelling on the real world.

The day passed in a haze of intermittent sleep and escapist literature, keeping shame at bay. Other than bathroom breaks and quick trips to the kitchen, I stayed safely sheltered in my bedroom.

The thought of admitting defeat sat like lead in my stomach. Several people had committed to help me, many already paid for flights. There was no relief in this surrender, only guilt and pain.

This would be the first time in my life I was going to DNS a race, a running abbreviation for "did not start." I had started and finished every race I'd attempted, a matter of pride I was only now acknowledging. I was not a quitter, it went against everything I'd been selling my whole life. Yet I was facing overwhelming odds, so stepping away was the right thing to do. No matter how logical the decision was, I could not find peace in my soul.

As evening approached, my phone rang. Looking down, I saw it was Joy, my daughter. She was twenty years old, living in the far eastern side of Washington State, while she was attending college. She had long, straight brown hair, clearly inherited from me, and beautiful green eyes she got from her mother. My youngest, she was usually positive and very quick-witted.

My son, Chris, and I referred to her as "the sniper" in our family. While he and I would banter, jest, and cajole each other endlessly, she would just sit quietly. Then, out of nowhere, she would lob out a comment that was so well executed it left us floored.

Like the time we were all getting ready to go on vacation just a few years ago. I was telling them about the hotel and amenities. To be funny, I added in at the end, "It will be a lot of fun, but if you come to visit my room and you see a sock on the door, well..."

My son gave the exasperated "oh my god" sigh with accompanying eye roll I expected, while Joy, without missing a beat, said, "Dad, if it ain't happening here, it ain't happening there."

After a brief moment of stunned silence at the unexpected hard truth, we all burst out laughing. She was ninja-level at finding those moments of humor.

Why is she calling?

I'd told her I would be gone and unreachable all weekend as I transformed into a mountain-running demigod. I didn't want to talk to her, I didn't want to talk to anybody. I could easily let it go to voicemail. I shouldn't be here. I'd spent the last twenty-four hours isolated in my bed and wasn't ready to face the world yet, but guilt won out. "Hello," I managed in a creaky voice that hadn't spoken aloud for a few days.

"Hi Dad!" she responded happily.

"What's up, is everything okay?"

"Yeah, great. Why?"

"I didn't expect to hear from you. I'm supposed to be out running all weekend."

"Oh, that's right! I forgot. I just felt like calling. How's it going?"

I paused, my mind spinning like a broken compass. I could make something up. Say I was between runs, or on the trail, or perhaps invent some technical difficulty that didn't involve my complete inadequacy. The silence lengthened as my mind spun. None of that felt right. I didn't want to confess, but the alternative was to lie. This was the moment of truth, I needed to rise to it.

"It didn't go well." Another pause, then the dam burst. "There was snow, so I had to change things up, but that didn't matter really because wherever I was, I wasn't able to keep the pace. I was going too slow and struggling. It was a lot harder than I thought. I had to stop and come home. It doesn't look like I can do it. I'm withdrawing from the race."

There. The truth, naked and shivering in the light. I felt all the pent-up emotions releasing like pressure from the now gushing waters, not with relief, but a torrent of pain, grief, guilt, and shame. I'd been sitting in emotional purgatory, and now that the words were out, I couldn't hold back the flood.

"That makes sense, I get it," she said with the kind of empathy that makes a parent realize their children might be wiser than them.

We sat silent on the line. I was torn up with emotions, nothing else to say. Her dog, Luna, barked in the background.

"Do you want to talk about it?" Joy asked.

"No. I can't... Not yet. I've been lying around in bed since I got home yesterday. You're the first person I've talked to, and I almost didn't answer. Maybe in a few days, but I just can't right now."

"All good, I get it."

Another long pause. My mind desperately sought conversation that didn't involve running, coming up as empty as this weekend's promise. All I could think about was how I'd let people down, how this exchange wasn't going poorly, but didn't feel great either.

There would be several more just like it, including with Jenni. A prospect I faced with all the enthusiasm of a root canal. What I feared was her quiet, supportive response carrying an undertone of judgment and shame. That was the worst.

"Hey, just a thought." Joy interrupted my spiral into self-pity.

"Yeah?"

"You should go run tomorrow."

I paused. Had she heard what I just said? Maybe that was why she was being so understanding and supportive. She had somehow missed the punchline.

"Why? I'm not training anymore. I'm not doing the race," I replied.

"I didn't mean for training. I meant just because. For fun. You don't have to go far or for long. Hike if you don't feel like running. Just get out there. You used to enjoy running, so just go have fun!"

Fun? That was something I had stored away along with other concepts like work-life balance and eight hours of sleep.

I didn't want to go run, or hike, or do anything but stay in bed, depressed, processing my failure. But I couldn't tell her that.

"Sure," I said with feigned enthusiasm. "Maybe I will."

"Think about it, see how you feel in the morning."

"I will, promise," I said sincerely.

It wasn't a lie. I would think about it. Then decide not to.

We hung up a few minutes later, and I rolled over, back to my book, seeking literary anesthesia. I shouldn't have talked to her, I wasn't ready to be social. Thankfully, I slept deep and well again that night.

I awoke with the sun after thirty-six hours in bed, feeling like Rip van Winkle. It was Monday morning, but work was still two days away thanks to the Fourth of July holiday. None of my clients were working, so I got a bonus day off. For the first time in weeks, if not months, I felt rested. Not just physically, but mentally too, like someone had hit the "reset to factory settings" button on me.

The driving fear was gone. The pressure of the race, work, family, and relationship expectations had lifted like morning fog. By quitting, I had relieved myself of a weight I didn't know I'd been carrying, though the crash landing had laid me out for a day and a half. I had not realized just how badly I needed rest until this moment.

Maybe I would listen to Joy after all. I wasn't going to do the race. That ship had sailed, sunk, and been declared lost at sea. This was simply a chance to move a bit, to run like I used to, without pressure. No clock, no distance, no goal except to remember why I'd fallen in love with this crazy pursuit in the first place. For fun.

It had been a long time since I ran simply for the joy of it. Perhaps getting out again would help me come to terms with how I felt. After all, I did my best thinking in the forest. At the least, I would be doing something other than laying here, and might keep the pending flood of emotions at bay a little longer.

For eight months, I had been pushing my body to greater lengths, constantly increasing distances and times. Every three weeks was a planned recovery week with easier workouts to let the body rest and rebuild, yet none of them had offered relief because I never slowed down enough to recover as I should have.

Now, after truly resting for the first time in months, my mind was fresh, and energy flowed through my body like it had been unclogged. Muscles were not fatigued and worn, but moving with ease. Today was going to be a good day, full of beautiful trails and absent the tyranny of training. I loaded up what I needed for a short run and headed out.

Rather than travel to some remote, technical trail, I opted for the twenty-minute drive to Forest Park, a decision that felt almost rebelliously practical. The park wound through the small mountains lining Portland's west side, where the Wildwood trail meandered over thirty miles like a particularly indecisive snake. I had no plan other than to go until I felt like turning around, likely only a few miles.

It didn't take long before I found my groove, moving at a pace that felt good rather than prescribed. I would power hike up hills, run downhill, and cruise the flats at whatever speed felt natural. Revolutionary concepts! The miles ticked away well ahead of the pace required to finish the Bigfoot 200. Not that it mattered. I had quit. Still, I couldn't help but notice that even though, admittedly, this trail was easier, I was practically floating.

Running had always been meditation for me, a moving prayer where my body went on autopilot, and my mind could wander. There I would find the magic place only experienced runners know, often referred to as the runner's high. A euphoric state of well-being that often came with a sense of calmness or exhilaration, attributed to the release of endorphins. It is different for everyone and rarely the psychedelic experience the uninitiated imagine. For me, it was a meditative state where thoughts could rise to the surface without anxiety, where I could sit with ideas like old friends.

In this space, I resolved work issues, exercised creativity, and worked through my relationship struggles. This was one of the reasons I loved running. It was not a headspace I could make happen, and it wasn't guaranteed with every run. It took longer miles to settle in, but if I could relax into the movement and let go of my mind, it would usually get there.

For the last few weeks, especially on those two brutal training runs, this space had been locked away like a room I'd lost the key to. Today, my mojo was back, flowing as steadily as the trail beneath my feet.

The forest here was lush and green, complete with large ferns carpeting the ground, moss clinging to bark like nature's graffiti, and trees rising to the sky with the confidence I aimed for. I felt like I could just keep running and never stop.

Reality knocked on the door of this peaceful moment like an unwelcome guest. I would have to stop eventually, turn around, head home, talk to people. Admit my defeat to Jenni. It was a sobering thought, but in the moment, I felt like an observer of my own life, which defanged the negative emotions. Objectively, it shouldn't matter what other people thought. The reality was that I did care. A lot. I especially cared what Jenni thought.

Why do I care what others think?

The answer came immediately.

Because I want to be loved.

This was a gentle slap of realization. I was constantly seeking her approval in the same way I sought it in previous relationships. In the way I yearned for it from friends and family. I knew this at my core, though I pretended I was beyond caring what other people thought. I had gotten pretty good at it too.

On a darker level, however, lurked a deeper truth. One I tried to not even acknowledge. Today, it managed to slip through the cracks of my psyche. I had a hard time accepting praise. Positive comments, what I craved most, washed quickly over and past me like a slipstream of air. They stood little chance of being heard, and even less chance of getting inside my head and finding a place to nest.

Because of this, the more critical of me others were, the more I trusted and believed the rare compliments. When they judged me, it reaffirmed negatives I already thought about myself. In contrast, moments of praise felt sincere. They saw the worst in me, so this meant the good must be true. If, as critical as they were, they could somehow love me, maybe I could love myself.

When I looked at it objectively, I could see it was a false equation, a paradox. Yet it had ingrained itself into my belief system. I feared what removing it might do to the world I had built around this premise, so instead I buried it deep.

There was too much truth in this moment. More than I was ready or willing to address. I thought of Linda, a woman I'd dated years ago who turned out to be addicted to pain pills. Seeking help, I'd gone to an Al-Anon meeting, a support group for the friends and family of addicts.

As I sat there listening to people share their stories, including one woman who spoke about how she had to end her marriage, I recognized that acknowledging Linda's addiction meant I would have to do something about it, up to potentially ending our relationship.

I did what any emotionally mature adult would do. I pretended everything was just fine until, just a few short months later, it inevitably wasn't.

Today is not the day to determine who decides I'm worthy of love.

I wasn't ready for this level of self-excavation. As I ran into a brief clearing where the sun broke through the canopy, I released the thought. It would return, like all important insights I wasn't ready to face. Maybe next time I would be brave enough to wrestle with it.

Lost in my groove, I suddenly realized I'd been running for over fifteen miles. Forest Park offered endless trails, but very few water sources. A design flaw I was well acquainted with but hadn't thought would be a problem to solve for today. This morning, I couldn't imagine going more than a few miles, so I didn't bring any nutrition and only minimal hydration. Food wasn't an issue—I never ate solid food while running, no matter the distance—but with water low already, I'd have to turn back.

Running further would just make the problem worse, though I felt a pang of regret. I had more miles in me, a thought both thrilling and ironic.

As I turned around, I checked my watch. Still well ahead of the pace needed to finish the race. Why did I care? The previous two days proved I wasn't ready. Might never be. But the numbers were interesting in the way that irrelevant statistics often caught my interest.

The miles started clicking off again as I headed back, my pace still strong. I felt a wave of gratitude for my daughter Joy. She'd known exactly what I needed to hear, throwing out the suggestion, knowing I wouldn't receive it well in the moment. Her wisdom gave me permission to let it all go, to remember that running could be fun rather than just another way to punish myself for not being enough.

I'd always been the one to help, to carry others across whatever finish line they were approaching. Now I'd been given permission to release the impact of my failure on others, to shrug that weight off my shoulders, to run lighter than I had in months.

The GPS pinged mile twenty as I drank the last of my water. Twelve long miles left to go, and I was already feeling thirsty from conserving what little I'd had.

Don't think about it.

I immediately focused on it with the precision of a laser beam.

Anxiety started to creep back in. I began to reflect on the first time I heard one of my younger brothers say, "You were like a father to me."

It surprised me. I was the second-born of eight children, and I hadn't felt like a dad in any way. I did not dole out discipline. I didn't provide for them or try to manage their lives. None of the things I imagined a father should do.

I was just being a brother, loving them, playing with them, helping where I could, and being present. Offering a listening ear, advice when appropriate. They needed guidance, someone to believe in them and cheer them forward. I was a presence of love and support, what kids really need from their dad, something I never had.

I had only briefly known a stern, cold presence before our father left. I was less than they needed, but sadly more than many kids, including myself, ever have. It felt good to hear they believed I provided this for them. Humbling and terrifying too.

Unintentionally, this added another layer of pressure on me to be strong. A brother could make mistakes, but I believed that a father figure had to be flawless. An impossible standard that I'd carried like a mountain on my back, from my brothers and right into actual fatherhood.

Talking about being tough wasn't enough, I had to show it. To run these long distances. To play down the fact I had several stents in my heart. To brush away failed relationships. To never show the fear that ate me up inside or the anxiety that drove me relentlessly forward. I couldn't show this side to my brothers, nor to my children as they grew up.

Thirst was nagging at me, pulling me from therapeutic gold-digging. Mile twenty-two chimed. Ten miles left, temperatures warming, and me having once again ignored basic survival needs in favor of momentum. Some patterns die hard.

Then, like a mirage that had me blinking several times to verify it was real, I saw them. Three gallon-sized jugs of water. Trail magic, left by runners who understood the unspoken code. If you had something another needed, you shared. Trail running community distilled to its essence.

I ran up to the jugs, found one that was still sealed, and refilled my hydration bladder with the reverence of someone receiving communion. This was a gift. After chugging down water greedily before topping off again, I headed back out with renewed confidence and a restored faith in the kindness of strangers.

Perhaps I could complete the Bigfoot 200. The thought drifted through my mind like a dangerous whisper.

Maybe just start and see what happens?

I hadn't told anyone but Joy that I'd quit. I hadn't officially withdrawn from the race, that unpleasant task was scheduled for later this week. What if, just maybe, I lined up at the start and saw how far I could go?

The furthest I'd gone before was 103 miles. Just one step farther would be an accomplishment. The Lewis River aid station, scene of my first training day tragedy in the mountains just a couple days ago, was at mile 112. Making it that far would be a victory no one could deny me.

In this moment of dawning optimism, I remembered a talk a coach had given the team the night before a race. I never forgot what he said, repeating it later when I coached teams of my own.

"Before any event," he said, "especially their first, most people are very nervous. First-timers often focus solely on finishing. Others, usually the more experienced, have time goals they want to hit. Before worrying about finishing or time goals, you each must first have the courage to start."

As I made my way back along the trail, I wondered if I could find that courage. To line up with everyone else that morning, reach the first aid station, and then the next, until I made it to Lewis River. Once there, I could see how I felt. Maybe I'd unearth the stamina to keep going, or maybe I'd go home knowing I'd gone further than ever before. Either way seemed like a win.

The last miles flew by, devoid of additional insights, but I'd had plenty today. Something had shaken loose in the recovery. I got back to my car feeling good, the sun still high, and my system hydrated. I'd started with the possibility of five or six miles, maybe ten at most. Instead, I'd covered thirty-two and could have done more.

I will hit the trails again tomorrow, I decided, *and see what the day brings.*

5

It was Tuesday morning, the Fourth of July. According to my original plan, I should have been recovering from a successful training weekend. Instead, I was out for a run. Not the snow-buried Bigfoot 200 course I'd abandoned, but a challenging trail an hour from home that had become my proving ground, chosen for its difficulty and technical conditions.

Alone in the woods, I was happy in my sanctuary. The one place I felt I could truly be myself, with no outside voices to correct me. Here, anxiety was absorbed by wilderness, thoughts untangled through rhythm, until I found whatever peace was possible. I paused briefly to watch snowmelt from higher elevations cascade over granite worn smooth by 10,000 such springs at the biggest waterfall on this trail, just over a mile in.

The Hamilton Mountain trail is a nine-mile loop that started with three miles of constant, steep climbing. This first section includes waterfalls and gorgeous Douglas firs with cathedral trunks rising 200 feet, their ancient bark ridged like armor. These giants gave way at the peak, overlooking the beautiful Columbia River Gorge nestled below Mount Hood's snow-crowned summit.

Most people turned around here to go back down, but for me, this view started the middle section, which wound behind the mountain with rolling hills threading through old-growth western hemlocks and red cedars that had been seedlings when Lewis and Clark paddled the river below.

The final three miles plunged down the other side over rock and root, back to the trailhead.

I didn't have a plan beyond motion itself, though the Bigfoot 200 percolated in the back of my mind. Today could test whether my pace through tough terrain would be enough, even though I was telling myself it was a run without expectations or goals. As the sounds of the waterfall faded, it was all about getting on the trail and having a good day.

My pack rode heavy on my shoulders, filled to the brim with water and nutrition. Even though today's run would be shorter, made up of loops with a water source every nine miles, I wasn't going to make the same mistake as my last disasters. It also still held all my race gear because I hadn't taken the time to unload anything.

Today felt buoyant, with controlled breath, steady energy, and my body flowing between run and power hike as terrain demanded. The few holiday hikers I passed seemed distant and irrelevant to this private negotiation between trail and self.

The trees welcomed me, ancient sentinels that had survived fires and countless Pacific storms. Every now and then, I would reach out a hand and gently slide my hand along the bark as I eased by, imagining energy exchanged, always receiving more than I gave. This ritual had formed early in my trail running, and the practice really helped late in a trail race. When I was tired and hurting, if I connected with a tree like this, I would get a small boost to revive me for a brief moment. Perhaps all that time alone in the woods brought out the pagan in me. It paired well with my adopted PNW flannel and beard.

At the peak, clarity stretched for miles. Sun warming my face as I took in the gorgeous view, a question bubbled up.

Can I find happiness in this moment?

I paused to consider the honest answer.

Yes, in this moment, I can.

This was quickly followed by another question.

What about the other moments?

Harder territory. I sipped on my water before continuing on the trail, leaving the question suspended behind me in mountain air.

Just weeks ago, we'd celebrated Jenni's birthday. I gave her a bracelet she'd coveted for several months while we were dining out, and she loved it. When I presented her with a birthday card during dessert, her entire mood shifted for the worse. I'd clearly mis-stepped somewhere.

"What's wrong?" I ventured, unsure where this was going to go.

"Nothing." Her typical first response, she always made me ask at least twice before surrendering the truth.

"No, really, what's wrong? You don't seem happy."

"Look at this!" She thrust the envelope forward, like a lawyer presenting damaging evidence in a case.

Before I even looked, I knew I was in trouble. If she gave in after only one "nothing," she was angry. The smaller the problem, the harder it became to get it out of her, and the more "nothing" answers I got. One nothing meant genuine anger.

I glanced down at the envelope where I had written "Jenny Bunny" as a fun play on her name. I couldn't see anything wrong. After a reasonable amount of time searching, I looked at her with an inquisitive look of ignorance.

"My name is spelled with an 'i' on the end," she said, tight-lipped.

"I know. I changed it to a 'y,' so it would end the same as 'bunny.' I thought it was fun, just playing around, trying to be cute."

Obviously, I knew how she spelled her name. The word play was obvious and deliberate. I'd spelled her name correctly inside the card, after all. She knew me better than this, didn't she?

"That's how my friend Jenny spells her name." It came out accusatory.

"Yes, I know. But the card is for you. I wasn't thinking about Jenny at all. I thought you might like it. Like when I added 'ing' to your name to rhyme with 'loving' for Valentines..." I drifted off, it was clear my rambling explanation wasn't helping, so I finished with a rushed, "I'm sorry."

I'd played with variations on her name before, and she'd always liked it. I only changed a letter in her name. I thought it was very clear that the card was intended to celebrate her. Yet here I was facing a conviction of literary adultery. She was cold to me the rest of the night. I remained baffled.

The next morning, she was happy, acting as if it had never happened. I didn't have the courage to probe into her behavior. She never explained nor apologized.

These were the moments that gave me doubt about our relationship, that made me question if I was happy and if this is what I wanted. It was why I had been delaying moving in together, despite us both wanting it. Moments like this didn't happen often, but frequently enough, I feared they would become my everyday life.

I feared living together and waking up each morning to her observant eye. I would straighten the bed, only to be told the sheet corners weren't tight enough. Maybe a throw pillow was two inches off center. The duvet cover revealing one too many wrinkles.

I envisioned making toast for myself at breakfast, the bread browning to what I considered perfectly golden, only to hear her voice from behind "That's too dark." I'd pop out the slice, start fresh, watching carefully this time. "Now it's too light," she'd say, arms crossed. A third attempt might earn grudging acceptance, but by then the coffee's cold and my appetite gone. The simple act of preparing breakfast, one she wouldn't even be eating, would become an anxiety-inducing negotiation.

Eventually, this scrutiny would follow me to work as she sat off to the side, listening to every interaction. "You spent too much time socializing, you need to get down to business in your meetings sooner," she might say. Or "That deal should have closed a long time ago. Why didn't you just get the contract signed?"

It would burrow into every facet of my life. Like how I tied my running shoes, double knots were excessive, single knots were irresponsible. The Superman emblem on my pajamas was childish, not for someone my age. Even how I breathed would eventually come to judgment under this fear.

It was all an extreme scenario, I knew. An unlikely slippery slope dissension into hell, yet I couldn't dismiss it as impossible that one day my every mundane action would require justification, explanation, and apologies.

I didn't want things to end. I loved her. And, it was difficult to admit, I had come to depend upon her to validate me. Someone so critical of the world around her, with such strong opinions, had chosen me. This meant I was desirable. If she left, who else would want someone like me?

Yet if she stayed, could I endure?

Three miles passed during this rumination, I realized as I turned onto the fire road to take on the downhill section. I relished the swift descent back to my car. I may have to haul my linebacker body up these hills, but gravity became a gift on the way down.

During runs, I processed these hard moments, usually coming to peace by the end. I would forgive rough moments like the birthday card and refocus on all the many good things in our relationship.

Doubts are just part of being in a relationship, right?

The truth was that Jenni and I communicated better than my previous relationships. More importantly, when I did find the courage to express my needs, she listened. Like the time we sat down to watch one of my favorite mini-series, "Dr. Horrible's Sing-Along Blog." Admittedly, a nerdy deep cut, but I was excited to share it with her, cuddled on the couch together.

Five minutes in, she said, "This is stupid, turn it off."

At first I thought she was kidding, but when I glanced over it was clear she wasn't.

"What's wrong?" I asked.

"I don't like it," she said flatly.

"But it just started. It gets better," I said feebly, thinking it was already great.

"Nope. It's dumb. Let's watch something else."

For once, I found the courage to speak up.

"I understand this may not be your thing," I said in as controlled a voice as my hurt ego could muster, "but there are much better ways to say it. You could have said you're not in the mood, or that you weren't enjoying it. Calling it dumb and stupid feels harsh."

She looked at me, as if suddenly noticing I was there. She paused for a moment, then sincerely said, "I'm sorry if I hurt your feelings. I really don't want to watch it."

Jenni never dismissed my entertainment choices so bluntly again, though I rarely attempted sharing my favorites after that. The exchange left me questioning my own taste, classifying my interests as too "nerdy" for our shared space. I resorted to watching and doing things I wanted only when she wasn't around. Another reason moving in with her seemed scary, it would drastically reduce the time for me to do what I liked.

Still, I had to acknowledge that she did listen when I was brave enough to communicate my wants and needs. Between her hurtful comments, there was plenty of good conversation, laughter, and I truly felt loved. Death by a thousand little cuts, yes, but with kisses and band-aids between wounds.

It was becoming clear in this moment that it had become my perpetual pattern. Finding happiness in the present moment, while drifting in the bigger sense of my life without purpose.

As I opened my stride a little more, easing into the descent, this section offered respite. Long, straight, gentle downhill with minimal navigation required. Settling in, a realization crystallized. Finding happiness where I was no longer seemed sufficient.

What about where I want to be?

I'd been holding back on my relationship with Jenni because I knew I couldn't be happy living like this for the rest of my life. But I hadn't been doing anything to change it, either.

I'd been managing our relationship like a boat drifting at sea, weathering storms while seeking beauty in whatever each day brought. Not unpleasant, but directionless. Better to choose a destination and plot a course with intention than let the currents take me where they may.

I wanted to steer the ship, but it terrified me. Choosing a direction meant deciding, and decisions could lead away from safety, toward endings. Another failed relationship contradicted the image of strength and purpose I was trying to project. Drifting felt safer, with the bonus it allowed me to avoid difficult questions I wasn't prepared to answer.

As I came into the parking lot, I figured I would practice aid station strategy. Not for the Bigfoot 200, which I wouldn't be running, but just in general. Every organized race has aid stations for first aid, general support, and water. Some also have electrolyte drinks and possibly nutrition. The longer the race, the more they have available. Ultra marathons up to a hundred miles will include choices like fruit, cookies, trail mix, salty chips, or boiled potatoes. Though I wasn't sure my doctor would approve, they would also often offer candy and sodas for quick energy and caffeine boosts.

The 200-miler offered the equivalent of catering service. They cooked food to order, including pancakes, eggs, burgers, and burritos of myth whose legend was sung to the heavens by previous participants. Some aid stations would include tents for sleeping, with blankets. Additionally, designated locations would have "drop bags" that runners could hand off at the start line, with a change of socks, special treats, jackets, or anything else that could be anticipated.

I'd learned over time to start preparing in the mile or two before an aid station for what I might need. Water refills were always necessary. Consume calories and electrolytes, and restock anything I had eaten from my pack were mandatory. Trail etiquette demands zero litter, so I'd need to dump any garbage I had or carry it to the next one lest I risk the wrath of the Trail Gods.

It was always wise to double-check my headlamp was operable if there was a risk of nightfall. For the 200-mile race, I would check in to see if I needed a short nap. It seemed basic, but it became easy to forget something when tired.

I wasn't doing the Bigfoot 200, I reminded myself, but it had become a good practice anytime I ran. I was able to get everything done within a few minutes before turning around and heading back out, this time in the opposite direction. It would appear different traveling the other way to keep things from getting monotonous.

I still felt good, with plenty of energy. I allowed myself a time check. Still well ahead of the required pacing needed to complete the race. This was a tough trail, similar to event conditions. Solid proof I wasn't in as bad condition as I'd thought after the first two brutal days.

I soaked up the forest as I pushed my way up the mountain. I could hear a red-breasted robin singing in the canopy above, barely pausing for me to pass beneath. A Douglas squirrel screeched at me from a nearby branch, protecting his turf. A cotton-tailed rabbit darted off the trail, looking back at me accusingly for displacing her. Occasionally, a black-tailed deer would materialize and then vanish into salmonberry thickets. Only the wildlife, with the river's icy rush as soft background music, punctuated this profound quiet. It was calming, peaceful. I took a moment of gratitude for just being here.

At first, my mind stayed quiet, letting thoughts gently drift in and out. I contemplated a project at work, reminded myself to order a new comforter before guests came, and went over my grocery list. Then I started to think about my brothers. I had an older brother, James. Then there were four younger brothers, Peter, Sam, Jake, and Bobby. I'd always idolized my cool, older brother, while with my younger brothers, I still felt pressure to be the strong father figure they needed, even if I didn't know what that meant.

Without anyone to model behavior, I emulated my mother, staying strong at all costs. I carried this over into how I parented my own kids, and the pattern remained unbroken.

When I was in the hospital for my heart procedure, I'd had to be wheeled about while they ran tests, my kids following like little ducklings about the hospital. I was terrified, truth be told, but I couldn't let them see that, so I went into humor mode. When we were loading into the elevator, a sweet-looking couple squeezed to the side, allowing my wheelchair, the nurse pushing it, and my kids to scrunch into the cramped space.

As the doors closed, I looked at my nurse and said casually, "So the doctor thinks I'm highly contagious and it's definitely airborne?"

The nurse had a facetious look as he glanced at the couple. They froze for half a second to process what I said before they burst out laughing. We all had a good chuckle, and they wished me luck as they got out on their floor.

My entire stay was like this. Obnoxious jokes, banter with the hospital staff, and laughs with the doctors. I liked this aspect of me, but I was using optimism as a shield and hiding my fears behind it. Not just at the hospital, but in all of my life. This kept myself, my siblings, and my kids from having an honest and open conversation about what we were feeling. As a result, I spent the hospital stay holding everything inside while they held onto their own unresolved worries.

I firmly believe a positive attitude is best in hard situations. If something bad were to happen, I would rather have had fun and light moments leading up to it than be consumed by dread. I want people to remember a happy me, not the depressed, scared, and angry parts. I lived based on this inherited philosophy in all aspects. It worked in that people thought of me as a happy person, yet I knew, deep down, things were broken because I couldn't share the hard parts of my life. I didn't know how to fix it.

I was executing on the pattern my mother taught me, that I'd then practiced on my brothers, and perfected with my kids. I didn't want this anymore for any of us. I wanted us to be able to talk about the bad things, not pretend there was only good. I was holding the secret of this failed training weekend tightly. Worse, I'd made my daughter a co-conspirator. I was carrying too much and growing weary.

How much longer can you hold it?

I didn't know the answer, but I had to recognize it would not be forever, as I hoped. Even more importantly, I could see my kids now holding their burdens, and I did not want this for them. If I wanted my kids to have better lives and relationships, for them to share their fears and concerns with me so I could help them, then I needed to lead by example.

I hit this realization as I approached the top of the mountain for the second time. The sky remained a bright, beautiful blue as the sun shone down on me. I felt the warmth of it, pausing to stand there, arms outstretched to soak it in. I was thankful for the insights that often came to me while I was out here, the challenge was to take them out of the woods with me. It was easy to step right back into old habits when returning to the world. I took a deep breath before resuming my run, letting gravity take me down the remaining three miles of this loop.

I returned to the parking lot feeling light. There was no doubt I was going back out for a third loop as I went into "aid station" mode again. Move quickly but smoothly and get back out on the trails. It only took me a few minutes before I was on the steep incline, repeating the direction I had gone the first time around.

I stole a quick look at my watch. I estimated I would need to average, factoring everything such as sleep and eating in, under twenty minutes per mile to hit my goal of finishing under ninety hours. The cutoff was 105 hours, plenty of buffer time. So far, even with the steep inclines, difficult trail, stopping to take in views, and time to refill my water, I was close to twelve minutes per mile.

Long ago, I'd learned that I did best when I let go of everything and just went out and ran. My fastest triathlon happened when my watch broke. It was an old Timex watch, cheap when I bought it several years before, yet it had been loyal. It had been acting up, so in preparation for that event, I changed the battery.

Everything was looking good until, bobbing in the water with several hundred other athletes waiting for the swim to start, I looked at my wrist and saw the screen blank. A closer examination revealed it was full of water. I had to have made a mistake putting it back together, ruining the integrity of the watch. There was no backup, and a waterlogged watch was a poor excuse not to start, so I shook it off and started swimming with everyone else.

With nothing to tell me how fast I was going, to encourage me to pick up the pace or warn me to slow down, I had to trust my body. I'd put many miles on it by now, it probably knew what it was doing. I pushed when I felt good, slowed down when I needed to. Traveling by feel, letting the moment be my guide. I was concerned I would be too slow without a clock to push me, but instead of panicking, I just rolled with it. Hours later, I was shocked after crossing the finish to discover I'd raced a Personal Record, or PR. Without the pressure of a clock, I beat my previous best by several minutes.

Over the course of this long training weekend, I had started by putting immense pressure on myself the first two days. This was a big part of what mentally broke me and brought me to the point I quit the entire race. These past two days, without any purpose but to run, I was feeling great, and the miles were flying by.

As I ran under the canopy of trees, the sun ducked behind a cloud. I couldn't see it through the leaves above me, but I could feel the temperature get a little cooler and the world around me get a little darker. I was nearing the mountain peak for the third and last time today, just six miles to go.

I loved these moments running in the trees alone. They were gifts of peace that I found nowhere else. Here was where I belonged. The trees never judged, and I didn't have to prove anything to them. The trees, birds, and animals simply wanted to coexist in contentment. Here in the forest, I felt included, everywhere else, I felt like I was always struggling to belong.

It felt different from my day-to-day life, where I was constantly striving to be good enough. I craved the approval of others, especially Jenni. When things were going well, we were a great team, and we accomplished a lot. There were many reasons I loved her, and why I stayed. The criticism was hard, but there were plenty of good times in between.

This was what I always did, though. I refused to think about the challenges, always focusing on the good. Finding happiness in the moment, without any idea of where I was going. I didn't even know what I wanted.

I want unconditional, unwavering support.

I surprised myself with an answer.

I wasn't sure how Jenni was going to react when I told her about my failure this weekend, she could be unpredictable. She might be sympathetic and caring. It was also possible she would lean into an "I was right, you shouldn't have tried this" attitude.

In contrast, my daughter Joy always listened, supported, and encouraged me, as she had on our phone call two days before. She wanted me to do the things that made me happy. She once said, "If you told me you were going to make an album of 80s rock ballads, I wouldn't doubt for a second it would happen."

In honesty, this was not a quality assessment, but rather faith in my commitment to completion. Such a difference from Jenni, who would catalog all the reasons I shouldn't. That my voice wasn't good enough would be of top mention. She'd have problems with its marketability, claiming "No one would buy it." Then there was the cost of recording, hiring a band, and producing it. She wouldn't be wrong.

Yet despite all the facts, I wanted someone who believed in my terrible 80s rock ballads album, that I could do it. I had zero expectations she would listen to it on repeat. I didn't want false praise. I just wanted someone who would support whatever crazy dreams I chose to pursue. It wasn't the first time this thought had surfaced, but today it resonated deeply.

On the other hand, I didn't want to be alone. I'd crossed the finish line with no one waiting for me too many times. Watched as others celebrated with loved ones while I took the long, lonely walk back to my car. I didn't want to go back to that.

I feared a life of constant examination, each little act under scrutiny. I dreaded an empty life with no one to share it. That's how I ended up struggling to maintain a position somewhere in between, caught in limbo. It wasn't the dream scenario, but it allowed the relationship to survive another day.

I accelerated slightly, wanting to outrun these heavy condemnations of my romance. It was a good day. A sense of peace like I hadn't had in months, vindication through long miles for a second day on technical terrain. My confidence had been shaken, but now it surged back. I was coming upon the final three miles of the day, relaxing into these downhill miles. With confidence, hope was returning, and things started to feel possible.

The pre-race pep talk my coach had always given us, that I'd adopted when I started coaching, came back into my mind. Whatever their goal, most people go into a race with a set of expectations, and I was no exception. The rest of his talk offered an alternative set of priorities to consider.

I heard Coach Craig in my head, just as it had been years ago, saying, "The first thing we should strive for is not to finish, but instead to have the courage to start. The majority of people never even take the first steps to begin such an endeavor, so just starting the race is a win in and of itself.

"Your second goal should be to stay healthy. Don't take unnecessary risks and listen to your body. If you need to slow down or stop, then do so.

"The third priority should be to have fun, to enjoy what you are doing. Take a moment to look around while you are out there, to soak up the views. No matter how much you may be hurting, find a smile.

"Fourth goal is to finish the race, to trust your training and your mind to get you through to the end.

"Finally, and only after everything else, should anyone worry about specific time or performance goals."

Just like not focusing on my watch helped me go faster during the triathlon, taking the stress off finishing created safer, more enjoyable events. When nervous about a race, I focused on the start line, staying healthy, and having fun. The rest always took care of itself.

Yet, the enormity of 200 miles and the resulting performance anxiety had blinded me to the first three principles. Obsessing about finishing had eliminated fun, driven my body toward breakdown, and made me forget that just starting was a win. As the trees flowed by, I considered what I had learned to help me get through previous challenges.

Coach Craig offered five principles, but I needed my own framework for this unprecedented distance. His first three principles remained relevant, as evidenced by my breakdown. For such a huge goal, I needed something more than time goals and finishing to get me through. By the time I was finishing the last loop, I had created what I called my *Six Steps to Completing Your 1,000-Mile Journey* that I believed would help get me across the finish line.

The concept was a set of tools to conquer an overwhelming, seemingly impossible goal, such as the Bigfoot 200. The title came easy once I decided to call them "steps" instead of principles, to go along with my running theme. A huge task simplified? Look no further than the Chinese philosopher Lao Tzu, who infamously said, "The journey of a thousand miles begins with a single step." I thought it was a fun play on his wise words.

My version, however, would be my own, based on my recent experience. I would keep Coach Craig's first principle, to take the first step. When I first heard this during his pre-race pep talk, he called it "the courage to start." At the time, it was a no-brainer for me. Of course, I was going to start. However, I recognized the value of this wisdom after surviving this difficult training weekend.

I would keep his second principle for my second step, to stay healthy. With a little perspective, I could see a big part of why this weekend had fallen apart was because I wasn't taking care of myself like I should have. Physically, I was running my body into the ground and not resting properly, while mentally, I was loading myself with expectations. Exhausted and weighed down, I was not managing my health well.

His third principle had proved to also be a keeper, to have fun. I had to admit I'd lost sight of the joy in what I was doing a long time ago. It had once been a release, a place I could let go. With all the pressure and expectations I'd put on myself, it had become a burden. I had to force myself out the door, and my happy place had become a slog of anxiety.

This is where I departed Coach Craig's principles, because time goals and finishing felt too distant for this. Yes, I wanted to finish and had a goal, but focusing on these at any point did not seem a means to success when the finish line was so far away.

Instead, my fourth step was to take it in segments. I needed to focus on what was in front of me, on getting through this moment, making it to the next aid station. The full racecourse felt overwhelming, but when I looked at each leg, it felt doable. Breaking things down into manageable pieces turned an impossible project into bite-sized, realistic pieces.

From experience, I knew step five would have to be to adapt. The bigger the goal, the task, or the journey, the more likely something will go wrong. Often several somethings.

A big part of endurance sports was to be ready for not if but when things fell apart. I'd done well this weekend initially, changing when the weather blocked the roads, but then I'd locked myself into the plan and pushed forward through all the signs I should pause and reassess.

My final step was to visualize the finish. If I couldn't imagine myself crossing the finish line, then I didn't believe it possible. The odds for success dropped quickly from there. Conversely, if I could see it in my mind, I became much more connected to the long-term goal. Even if only for the moment, it felt real. A reminder the finish would be worth the price I was paying to get there. When I saw myself triumph, it became more than just a dream, but rather a prediction of the future.

Back at my car, I changed my clothes with gusto, pumped up the seat warmers, and relished my new plan. I was going to at least toe the start line of the Bigfoot 200. I would have the courage to start, then see what happened. It felt good, like I was myself again.

Driving home, I called Joy.

"Hey, so I've been out running the past couple days, and it felt great!" I told her after our hellos.

"That's awesome, Dad! I'm so glad." She didn't sound surprised.

"And, well, I'm thinking I may try and start the race. Dunno how it will go, but I should at least start. I've come this far."

"Sweet! That's good. Just have fun and see what happens!" she replied with an audible smile.

I suddenly suspected she knew this would happen when she encouraged me to get back out there, but I didn't ask. I was just grateful for the gift she had given me, a restored joy in running and the hope I might finally outrun the demons that had been chasing me for so long.

I decided to tell no one else about that weekend's defeat and race withdrawal. I could keep it to myself and escape any shame and doubt, maintaining the illusion that the weekend was a success because, truly, it was.

Unpacking at home, I spread any gear that wasn't going into the washer to dry before heading to the bathroom. A long, hot shower after a trail run is one of my favorite things. Standing under the water, watching dirt slither down the drain, I felt satisfaction replace the previous days' suffering without purpose. The last two days felt like I was edging into the space of endurance, demonstrating strength with intent and accomplishing more than I thought I could.

With five weeks to go, I refocused my training with less pressure on myself. I enjoyed my runs and rested when I needed to. The final few weeks were a taper, decreasing distances to allow full recovery so that my body would peak on race day.

"How'd the training go?" Jenni asked the following weekend after she'd returned from her trip.

"Great, got in some good miles." Truth, I rationalized.

"Nice," she replied with a distracted delivery as she unpacked.

"Tell me more about your trip!" I encouraged, to change the topic.

She proceeded to captivate me with her experiences in Bali. They'd of course hit all the regular tourist spots, but also discovered some rare finds. They even made friends with a local family and were invited over to dinner. I was jealous of her fun adventure and very glad she got to share this with her friends.

In the past, it wouldn't have felt good that she wasn't curious about my experience, but this time I felt grateful she didn't push for details. I didn't want to discuss my failure and expose myself as a potential fraud. Her lack of interest allowed both of us to maintain the illusion of my strength.

Few of my family or friends asked about the weekend either, and those that did accepted the same answer I'd given Jenni. Everyone assumed I'd conquered as usual, and I offered no contradiction. Their faith in me should have been reassuring, instead, it made me feel more alone. I was seeing why it's good to talk about the hard things.

As a distraction from nerves, Jenni and I finalized the race crew details. Crewing an ultra-runner was demanding work, earning its acronym CREW: Crazy Runner, Endless Waiting. One slightly insane person ran while the crew drove to the next station to wait, sometimes several hours, for the runner to catch up. The crew would lug supplies from the car to the trail and back, worrying during delays, hoping they hadn't missed the runner or forgotten essentials. Because they are so focused on the details and anxious about missing their person or making a crucial mistake, crews also suffer sleep deprivation, often forgetting their own needs to eat or drink. It is hard work that is greatly appreciated by the runner, especially this one.

To ease the burden, I over-prepared with printed directions and ensuring Jenni had a GPS navigation unit that worked off latitude and longitude, which was necessary to get to many of the remote aid stations. I bought snacks, drinks, and provided clean pillows and blankets for sleeping in the car.

As the race got closer, my relationship with Jenni improved. She rarely criticized, demonstrating excellent help and support in the final weeks. I didn't know why. Since we didn't talk when things were bad, I maintained the silence now that they were good. I hoped it meant she was finally proud of me because I had made it this far. All I needed now was a strong race performance, and everything would be perfect going forward. Naïve, but I allowed this hope to live.

Jenni became a super crew leader, organizing the people, supplies, and communication channels that would help me cross the finish line. One day, I saw her working diligently and leaned over her shoulder to see what she was doing.

"What? You created a whole binder?" I exclaimed.

"Yes, it's got everything. Maps. Contact info. GPS coordinates. Your estimated times. When people are arriving and leaving."

I was amazed. She had a tab for everything. The supplies I anticipated needing at each stop. My aid station checklist. Her own checklist of to-dos while I was out running. There was a tab for each section of the race, and one for each crew member with their specific instructions.

"You are freaking amazing," I said in wonder.

This was the type of support I dreamed of. Someone who went all in with me on my crazy adventures. Above and beyond what I expected. I felt a wave of love and appreciation for her. There had been a positive shift in our relationship, and I was enjoying every moment. Leaning into the good vibe, with the hope of encouraging it to continue, I sat down next to her so we could thumb through what she had created. I particularly wanted to review the crew information as it was fresh on my mind.

This included pacers, the folks who would meet me at an aid station and run with me for that section. Pacers couldn't "mule," or carry anything for their runner, nor assist in any way other than moral support. For runners with time goals, a pacer kept them on track. In my case, I looked forward to the company and welcomed distraction. Most importantly, they would keep me from getting lost or confused, especially if I hallucinated during the late miles of the race. This was common due to sleep deprivation and fatigue from running so much, a side effect of 200 milers.

My pacers included my son Chris, who was flying up from Central California. Kim was a good running friend, always up for an adventure, flying in from the San Francisco Bay Area. Jeff, whom I knew from a running club in San Jose, California, when I lived there, was also coming up. My good pal Keith, whom I had paced for the last fifteen or so miles of his hundred-mile run a few years ago, was joining me for some of the hardest miles, making the three-hour drive from Portland to help. My mom was traveling with my son to participate in a purely support role, and I was grateful to have her there.

As we continued through the binder, we came to Jenni's sections. In addition to leading my motley crew, I asked Jenni to pace me for two different sections. I'd met her through a running friend, and early in our relationship, she paced me during a fifty-miler I was running. I had come in tired and drained from the heat and hills, unsure I wanted to continue.

"You look great!" had been the first words out of her mouth.

I rose to the moment, lifted my drooping shoulders, and smiled. I could hardly say I was thinking about quitting when she looked at me with admiration and confidence. I drank some water then continued down the trail as she shared fun stories from her early running days. When she left me at the next aid station so she could meet me at the finish, I ran in gratitude with buoyed energy.

Since then, she had paced me for several other events, including one hundred-milers. I always asked her to be at sections I suspected I would be at my lowest because she always somehow found a way to pick me up. This time, in addition to a predicted low spot, she would be taking me the last thirteen miles to the finish line.

As the days went by, Joy never said anything about my bad training weekend, and I kept it under wraps too. She was away at college, uninvolved in the planning or running of the race, though she'd already played a huge part, as I wouldn't even be starting without her.

As a result of the experience, unnoticed by others, I changed how I talked about the Bigfoot 200. Instead of saying I was "running the race" or "finishing," I exclusively used the words "starting the race." A subtle shift, but combined with my new success steps, it greatly lowered my anxiety.

Quieted, but not gone, questions remained swirling in my head. Could Jenni support me for who I was and not who she wanted me to be? Or who I was pretending to be? Was our relationship changing for the better? Could it stay that way?

So much more than Jenni, here lay the crucible where I'd discover my worth as a dad, brother, son, and partner. Roles I'd performed with desperate approximation, never believing I was enough. Could two hundred miles through the wilderness finally silence the voices that criticized me, the demons that chased me? The trails would serve as judge and jury, indifferent to my fears but honest with their verdict. All I needed to do was make it to the start line, then hope the trails would judge me worthy.

6

At 4:30 AM, the alarm's assault began. Sometimes the hardest part of any race isn't the running, it's the brutal jolt of leaving a warm bed for a cold morning. To combat this, I didn't allow myself to hit the snooze button. I hadn't slept well, but that was normal for any runner's pre-race night. Going in already tired was part of the experience.

The Bigfoot 200 began at 9:00 AM, but two hours of driving plus an hour of built-in buffer time for my peace of mind meant we needed to leave very early. I was anxious enough without having to worry about being late.

Jenni and I climbed sluggishly into the car at 5:30 AM. With some forethought to avoid critical decisions while half-conscious, we'd already loaded up the night before. I sat in the driveway idling, giving both the engine and my mind time to warm up. A weight of departure settled over me. I wouldn't be back for three or four days. The world would continue its relentless spin while I battled on the trails.

The starting line was at Marble Mountain Sno-Park, the same place I'd decided to quit the race just a few weeks ago. Despite my recent attitude adjustment, I was not certain I was going to finish, and fear remained my reliable companion. To stay motivated, I was activating the first of the six steps I had created five weeks ago, focusing on taking the first step. I just had to have the courage to start the race, that's all I was focusing on.

This didn't change how tough the course was going to be. I hadn't forgotten how the trails destroyed me that training weekend. Jenni still didn't know of my previous defeat. Some failures are too raw to share, even with those closest to us. I let her assume I was just having normal race-day jitters.

We arrived around 7:30 AM as planned and sat in the car for about thirty minutes, attempting a failed nap. Eventually, I gave up and started getting organized.

My pack was stuffed with water, food, and the required cold-weather gear, night equipment, and emergency supplies. Some runners choose to pass their cold and night gear to their crew to lighten their packs, but I opted to have mine with me. I was genuinely nervous that something might go wrong. What if the crew got a flat? I'd be in big trouble without my gear.

With thirty minutes to go, it was time to get serious. I tied my shoes tight and checked to make sure everything was in place. I pinned my bib, number thirty-five, to my shorts. When registering, we could request the race number we were assigned, a rare treat, and I had chosen this one because it was my favorite number. As a young boy, I couldn't decide which I liked more, three or five, so, with the same gusto that would come to define me as I grew older, I chose both. The number thirty-five had adorned team jerseys throughout my younger years, and now I would carry it with me here too. Strapping on my pack, we headed to the staging area where the start line awaited.

Jenni and I joined the congregation of 189 other devotees. Runners milled around attempting to keep warm, deep in their minds, like nervous pilgrims before their voyage. Breath visible in the air, we all radiated palpable unease. Historically, at least sixty of us wouldn't finish the race. I tried not to calculate the odds that I would be one of them.

Despite obsessive course study, in this moment, I focused only on the first section. The fourth step I had developed to get me across the finish line was to take it in segments, and it was time to put that into action. No dwelling on the 206.5 miles ahead, only the upcoming 12.2 miles to the first aid station, which included 3,192 feet of elevation gain and 2,654 of downhill.

The Empire State Building, tip to base, measures over 1,400 feet tall. We'd climb and descend that distance more than twice in just this first section. Four miles up the side of Mount Saint Helens, two miles of rolling hills along the ridge, three miles down the other side, and then two miles of roller coaster hills.

Weather reports promised high nineties during the day, dropping into the forties at night. This was a giant temperature swing, but I had everything I needed, from sunscreen to warm layers. Sixteen hours of Pacific Northwest daylight this time of year meant the nights would only last eight hours. Smoke from distant forest fires hazed the air. Enough to notice, not enough to stop the race. Conditions weren't great, but they could have been much worse.

The morning chill bit through my shorts and technical shirt, but I'd warm up once we got going. Most of us shivered, suffering for the efficiency of not shedding layers a few short miles in. I welcomed the cold, memorizing its sharp clarity because soon enough, I'd be miserably hot in the sun.

Someone in a Sasquatch costume wandered around the starting line parking lot, a welcome distraction, at least for some of us. I got my picture taken with Bigfoot, killing a minute of the wait.

I could feel the anxiety circling like a vulture.

Just start! Get to the first aid station, you can do that.

Amelia Earhart once said, "The most difficult thing is the decision to act, the rest is merely tenacity," a quote I'd recently read during my training.

Tenacity, I had.

Strength.

I was an expert at enduring.

After quick announcements containing last-minute race details, we shuffled toward the starting line. I hugged and kissed Jenni. Several hours and many miles would pass before our reunion. Positioning myself toward the back, I hoped to avoid the inevitable carnage of middle-pack adrenaline. My strategy was slow and steady. Sprinting up a volcano at the crack of the starting gun wasn't part of any reasonable plan to avoid burnout.

The countdown with the race director began, and then we all surged forward under the inflatable arch and onto the trail. I ran faster than I should have, but it looked good for Jenni and the crowd. I would be out of sight within a few hundred yards. Plenty of time to slow down, catch my breath, and find my rhythm.

The early part of the trail accommodated five or six runners across, but soon it would narrow to single track, only wide enough for one person at a time. Over the next few days, we would spread out, the front and back ending up more than two days apart. We all wore mandatory GPS trackers, which allowed family and friends to watch our progress online, but more importantly, the race directors could locate wayward souls who'd strayed from the path or stopped moving entirely.

I kept a good, steady pace up the hill. Candice, the race director, had created unique trail markers she called "dragons." The pink and yellow reflective marking tape tied to clothespins resembled flames coming out of tiny dragons' mouths. The dragons were clipped to branches and bushes, clearly marking the path we should be on. It saved us from getting off course, especially where the trails split. An extra benefit was that they could be easily removed and reused for future races, minimizing waste.

Race day nerves notwithstanding, my anxiety remained manageable. There was no need to push myself faster, no constant fear eating up precious energy. The volcano's slope demanded respect. I breathed heavily but felt strong. At the first major split in the trail, I noted an absence of snow. During my previous attempt, several patches had already appeared by this point.

My body was taking its customary warm-up time. Some runners could sprint from the starting line feeling good. I needed a few miles of easy running before settling into a groove. Until then, I would be slightly out of breath, sluggish, and feeling heavy. I could feel my heart pounding from the exertion, each beat reminding me it had almost failed me. I imagined what was happening in my chest, visualizing the stents pulsing with blood. I was demanding a lot from my cardiovascular system to prove worthy of this undertaking, which sent a nervous pang through my gut. Could my heart do it?

To distract myself from neurosis, I studied my nearby fellow sufferers, wondering what each of their stories were. A young woman, barely twenty years old, seemed to skip with infectious joy. Just ahead was a muscled Marine veteran, his face steel determination. Behind me, a man in his late sixties smoothly jogged, his balding head sporting wisps of gray hair. The people I'd seen at the start line represented a wide range of ages and body types, each of us battling personal demons through voluntary hardship.

Many runners discovered community during a race, forging connections that could last from a few minutes to decades. I preferred solitude. The space to burrow deep within myself and examine the pain there. Fortunately, my pace usually naturally isolated me from others, providing the perfect balance of solitude in my mind and solidarity of the task ahead.

The climb continued into terrain I did not recognize from the training run. At first, I was worried, but then I saw a dragon marking the way. Looking around a little more intently,

I realized that just five short weeks ago, this entire area had been buried under several feet of snow. I'd been climbing over, falling through, and meandering my way across deep snow that had transformed the landscape entirely. What a difference five weeks made!

I knew from experience that constantly checking the distance I'd traveled would be like watching water come to a boil. To outsmart myself, I'd ditched my GPS watch for a cheap digital one that cost only ten dollars. I'd only know the time, not my pace. A quick glance revealed that even without precise calculation, I was well ahead of my last adventure here.

It did not feel very long before I emerged from the trees into the boulder field, without a single snowflake. The day's warmth built steadily, lava rocks now radiating heat back up into the air. Dragons weighted with stones marked the path from post to post. I confidently joined the conga line of runners, moving like ants across the landscape.

There was comfort in being a part of something bigger than myself. We were all trail runners who had spent many long months preparing to take on this challenge. While we would each have to do it on our own, the group's striving together boosted my spirit.

Cresting boulders the size of buses, I spotted the lava field's end ahead with green trees promising shade. As the woods grew closer, I acknowledged that here was where I'd admitted defeat. That day, the lava field had ended with no clear path forward. Today, there was no doubt which way to go. Stepping into the trees felt triumphant. I'd already exceeded my previous attempt in much less time. I'd only completed four percent of the race by this point, but I was starting to think there was a chance I would finish.

Don't get too confident.

My internal critic materialized right on schedule. While wisdom lay in avoiding hubris, I wondered if I was too harsh on myself. Confidence can bring strength, something I projected to others while internally harboring constant self-doubt. I felt the anxiety starting to creep in, pushing me faster.

In response, I took a deep breath and slowed down. Too early to unravel. In an effort to distract myself, I examined the forest's transformation. Lower elevation trees had been shorter, thirty to forty feet tall, more branched, and surrounded by ferns and other plants, providing bright green undergrowth thriving on the sun that penetrated to the forest floor. Here, at higher altitude, mostly branchless trunks reached up to a hundred feet or more, bursting above with canopies that filtered light to cathedral dimness. The ground lay littered with leaves, fallen trees, and other debris, but few living plants. It was darker and yet also more open.

Rolling hills replaced steady climbing. I found my rhythm, discovering relaxed comfort matching the surrounding silence. I used this time to recover from the uphill exertion and to let some of the anxiety go.

Soon, I noticed runners appearing and disappearing along a branch in the trail. The out-and-back to the Blue Lake aid station. I took the turn, covered the half mile or so, and cruised into bustling activity. My watch read 12:33 PM. Excellent time, hitting the front end of my expected window of arrival.

Runners, volunteers, and crew moved in a swarm, full of positive energy this early in the race, overflowing with optimism. I saw Jenni, and we quickly executed our aid station checklist. No food needed yet. No garbage to throw away. I wouldn't be sleeping here. Hydration pack and water bottles were topped off.

"Drink some electrolytes?" Jenni suggested.

"No, I'm good," I responded quickly.

"You should take some, it will be good for you," she encouraged.

"It's only been twelve miles, I'm fine," I insisted.

"Please?"

I felt resistance building, the familiar push-and-pull that had infected our relationship. Refusing to do what she suggested had become my small, unspoken rebellion against the way I perceived her as controlling at times. Perhaps because the pressure had been off the last few weeks, or maybe it was the processing I'd been doing while running, but in this moment, I felt a release.

"Okay," I said, with a smile.

She appeared surprised, then looked happy to be heard. When I wasn't fighting her guidance, I could see she was making a reasonable request, only wanting what was best for me. Drinking electrolytes would not harm me, it could only help.

This also served as an excellent reminder of the second step I'd developed, to stay healthy. There were many miles ahead of me, and I did not want to repeat past mistakes. I needed to maintain myself physically and mentally, starting before things got bad. I turned around and headed back to the hydration table.

"I understand you have some electrolytes here," I said in a jovial manner.

"That I do! You prefer them red, blue, or purple?" the aid station worker responded, matching my energy.

"Let's go purple today," I laughed.

He had long brown, curly hair. A full matching beard couldn't hide the huge smile. His green eyes shone brightly. Clearly someone happy to be here, and possibly anywhere. He was about my height and appeared to be a runner himself, as many volunteers were. He handed me a cup of purple drink.

"How you doing?" he asked as I chugged it down.

"Never better!" I grinned.

"I'm jealous," he said. "Wish I could be out running with you all!"

"You're welcome to take my place," I joked.

"Nah, I'm good, trust me." He grinned. "But I hope to run it next year."

"Awesome, you totally should!" I replied as I stepped away, reenergized.

Whether the electrolytes helped or not, the interaction lightened me. Such brief encounters can make or break one's mood, here as much as anywhere. Time spent in the aid stations counted against my total time, but the few seconds in conversation were worth the happiness I would carry with me over the following miles. Even my moments with Jenni had been positive, a meaningful difference.

Never one to linger at aid stations, seconds may not matter, but minutes added up. I thanked Jenni for being here and for the electrolyte suggestion. She beamed, appreciating the acknowledgment. After a quick kiss, I headed back to the main trail and turned left.

The next mile alongside a river was sublime. Rushing water provided a peaceful vibe and cooled the air. Trees offered mixed sun and shade, a perfect combination as the day's heat was intensifying. The shaded woods returned when the trail parted from the river as I made my way down the back side of Mount Saint Helens.

Ahead lay a tough 18.1 miles: 3,829 feet of uphill and 2,969 feet of descent. Downhill wasn't the joyride it could be perceived as. Out here, it often meant rocky terrain, loose soil, and steep, quad-destroying grades. This section had several long ups and downs, including one mile of particularly steep climbing. I couldn't forget the notorious rope climb down into and then up and out of a deep ravine. Most of this section would be sun-exposed during the hottest part of the day.

Eventually trees thinned, and I reached the ravine. The trail dropped nearly forty-five degrees and eighty feet to a rushing river at the bottom. A thick rope with knots every eighteen inches was anchored to a thick tree at the top. I peered over the edge to ensure there was no one on the rope.

Don't think, just do.

I grabbed the rope and started down, using the knots to slow me down as my feet rappelled along the cliff face.

Safely at the bottom, I joined a short line of other runners waiting to cross the river utilizing another rope that enabled a safe crossing as the cold water rushed over large, loose rocks. Mid-thigh deep, as expected. I'd hoped to keep my shoes dry a little longer, but it was inevitable.

When my turn came, I grabbed the rope and stepped into the icy water. Halfway across, I spied a photographer perched on a large boulder waiting to capture the perfectly adventurous moment. I paused to beam a broad smile for the camera before pulling myself across.

Another line formed for the rope going up to escape the ravine. A couple runners behind me started grumbling about delays and why multiple people weren't climbing simultaneously. Trail runners aren't known for complaining, but I understood the nerves and adrenaline flowing through us all.

I glanced over my shoulder and said, "I only want one person at a time because we don't know how much weight it will hold. It will also be harder to climb if it's getting pulled about in different directions. We're going to be out here awhile, a few minutes won't make a difference."

They fell silent as we watched the next few people climb up one at a time. When I was next, I waited until the person ahead was done before starting. I hadn't gotten more than ten feet when I felt the rope tighten, then start jerking around. Sure enough, the person behind me had jumped right on, deciding they weren't going to wait. As if one minute was going to make or break their multi-day run.

Frustration flared, yet there was nothing to do but continue. I considered letting myself slip a bit, accidentally kicking a foot back into them. Justice might be served, but it would be counterproductive. I was a better person than that, but the devilish idea lingered.

Clearly, the climb was harder for both of us, made worse when a third person jumped on after him. I got to the top, struggling against the taut rope, not bothering to look back. I let go of the irritation, grateful my higher self had prevailed. I was going to be out here for a few days, I had better things to do with the energy than waste it on them.

May the Trail Gods serve them the karma they deserve.

I grinned from the adventurous interlude, even as a trail run, this was extreme. Beyond the ravine, the few scattered trees provided insufficient shade. Early afternoon heat pounded me with a vengeance. I'd studied the topographical maps and the course description, but I should have gotten satellite images. What I encountered next looked like a literal desert. I was surrounded by sand dunes.

How? What?

I'd known large sections on the volcano's blast side would be barren, but I never imagined this.

A nearby runner complained about ash, which explained it. The surface was as soft and challenging to run through as loose sand, my feet slipping as I went. My shoes, still wet from the river crossing, collected the fine grit into a clinging mud. Temperature rising by the minute, it was difficult to spot the trail as we followed dragons clipped to rare patches of dead grass.

Up and down the dunes I plodded, unable to run, dripping sweat. I'd filled my water to the top, but it was going quickly as I kept drinking, trying to stay ahead of dehydration. My original 120 ounces had already dwindled to twenty. I tried to remember embracing the cold earlier that morning. It didn't work.

In the struggle, I found a brief moment of gratitude for Jenni making me drink electrolytes. It had been another good moment for us, one of many recently. It felt hopeful.

I knew I needed to talk to her about how her critiques made me feel. Things would need to change if we were going to survive. I wanted to work it out, but I wasn't good at hard conversations. I feared the consequences of mentioning things she didn't want to hear.

The topics were often mundane, but the rancor was real. A few months ago, Jenni started spending a lot of time at my house, laundry piling up for both of us. I never minded washing laundry, doing it every Monday, but I was notorious for putting off folding it, leaving it piled on the couch or a spare bed. Jenni had opposite habits, only washing when it absolutely had to be done. Her hampers were always overflowing, but she folded things as soon as they came out of the dryer.

When Monday rolled around, I washed her laundry to help her out. I left it on the couch as usual, with the intent of folding it in the afternoon, only to discover Jenni had folded everything. We fell into this pattern for the next several weeks, where I washed, and she folded.

One day, while she was folding, I chanced a request. Bravely, for me, which translated to timidly, I addressed how she folded the towels.

"Hey," I said delicately, "it's all good, whatever you want to do, and I won't ever mention it again, but I was wondering if I could ask you to fold the towels a little differently?"

She looked at me confused.

"When you fold them, I have to refold them to hang them over the racks in the kitchen and bathrooms." Demonstrating the way I folded, I continued. "If you fold them this way, then I can hang them easily, without requiring refolding."

I couldn't tell what she was thinking or feeling, she just looked at me with a blank stare.

"Anyway... again, all good... You do it however you want, I won't mention it again..." I drifted off, then stood there awkwardly for a moment, the little confidence I'd started with dashed, before walking away.

She started folding them my way, but two weeks later, when I mentioned I was going to be doing laundry, she blew up at me.

"You always wash the laundry, then make me fold it!" she yelled.

I was shocked. "I thought that was our agreement? That was just how we did it?"

"What are you talking about?" she asked, frustrated.

"I thought... but I..." I stammered, took a breath to slow down, then continued, "You don't really like to wash, I don't like to fold. We've been doing it this way, I thought we were good."

"I don't mind washing!" she said loudly. "You just always did it and left me to fold."

I was surprised at the outburst, she'd not said anything, and normally she would speak up.

"I'm sorry. I misunderstood." I paused, then, when she looked at me, expecting more, I continued, "We can figure something else out. I'm good with however you want to do it."

She looked disappointed, like I hadn't grasped her emotional pain. I didn't know what I was missing, so I stayed silent and waited.

"You're being controlling!" she finally blurted out. "Telling me how to fold the towels. I don't like it!"

At this point, I was completely confused because my mild request felt reasonable, and I gave her space to choose how she proceeded. There was no possible way I could interpret it as controlling, it was almost laughable. Still, I knew better than to laugh. I also knew challenging her would only lead to more conflict.

"I'm so sorry, I had no idea you felt that way, and I didn't mean for it to be like that," I apologized.

She appeared mollified, but not satisfied, with my answer, and we both left it at that. Maybe she had been controlled in the past, and my request triggered that. She didn't offer any more context, nor did I ask for any. I returned to doing only my own laundry and folding it too. An early domestic spat, poorly handled.

The desert section slowly gave way to an otherworldly, rocky landscape, no sign of life except the rare bird flying overhead. No color other than the grays and blacks of the rocks. Almost forty years since the volcano erupted, and yet this land remained lifeless. I remembered reading somewhere plants couldn't grow due to the acidity of the ash. I marveled at how much devastation had been unleashed by Mother Nature and how enduring its effects were.

The air remained hot and dry, in the high nineties, though it felt over a hundred degrees. At least the footing was firmer with the caked mud falling off my shoes. There were occasional breezes, and I resolved to thank the sun for its warmth and the wind for the cooling, trying to make peace with the world around me.

I slowed down to a fast walk, knowing my water wouldn't last. Endurance events are riddled with ups and downs, a big part of the challenge is about weathering the storm. Yet there are critical moments that will end the day. Becoming severely dehydrated would be one. With the worry, the darkness inside began creeping in.

I pondered again about the folding towels episode, which, combined with others, made me hesitant to broach larger topics. It wasn't just with Jenni, I'd been avoiding difficult conversations long before we met. I'd learned it young.

In a large family with lots of loud voices, I wasn't heard. It was not that feelings, wants, or needs were discouraged, there just wasn't any space for it. There was always someone louder, needier, or with a higher priority. If I tried to speak up, it got lost in the void. Either no one listened, or I was competing to be heard. In response, I learned to deal with whatever was happening alone. It was up to me to hear my problem, find a solution, and then make it happen. If no solution existed, I sucked it up and dealt with it.

From the darkness in my mind slid a memory with my older brother. Sharing rooms with so many siblings inevitably led to arguments.

"What'd you do to my stuff?" I yelled at James one day when I was twelve years old.

"Moved it outta my space," he answered nonchalantly.

"That's my space on my side of the room!" I continued yelling.

"Nope. Mine," he said with a knowing grin.

It had been my space until he decided he wanted it. We both knew it. Yet he played dumb while I grew angry and upset. He remained calm as I stormed out of the room in search of Mom, convinced she'd set the record straight.

I found her in the kitchen amid chaos. Dinner threatening to boil over, two-year-old Wendy crying in her arms, Bobby in tears at her feet, while Jake tried to explain why he was innocent of whatever wrong he was being accused of. Peter searched his backpack for something that required her signature while the phone kept ringing, unanswered. I was not going to get any help here.

Defeated, I returned to our room. James was absent, but I didn't dare reclaim the space. He'd simply take it back, more aggressively, emboldened by Mom's lack of interference. I sat on the bed, frustrated. No one to right the wrong. No one to listen. No outlet for any of my feelings. I felt even more incredibly alone than usual.

I probably wasn't the only one in the family who felt this way. My mom likely felt more alone than any of us. Yet we all reinforced that loneliness by not talking about it.

Searching for some access to power, I decided to run away. Perhaps that would teach them a lesson. At least it would give me some agency. I wrote a quick note explaining why I was leaving, left it on my bed, grabbed a few essentials, and headed out the front door.

Foreshadowing my future need to escape by running in the woods, and not knowing what else to do, I boarded the first bus that came along. I rode that bus until it stopped, then got on another, continuing for several hours. Eventually, I calmed down, and, recognizing the lack of a plan for where to go or what I was going to do when I got there, decided it was time to go back home. Figuring out a more direct route had me home in an hour.

I assumed everyone would be worried, but when I got back four hours later, no one even noticed I'd left. Briefly upsetting, but there was no one to discuss that with either. Without remedy, I surrendered the disputed portion of the room to my brother and moved on, not thinking about it again. Until today.

The sense of surrender, assuming no one would hear me, had poisoned past relationships, and my current one with Jenni too. Instead of expressing needs and wants, I held it inside. Managed it, processed it, fixed it all alone. Because these negotiations were one-sided and internal, I always conceded the situation to what it was. I never sought outside counsel, even a therapist, because I was programmed to think I was alone. There was no cavalry coming to save the day. Not even a single horse.

This approach kept the peace and allowed me to find happiness in the moment, but it wasn't healthy. It must have been difficult for partners to navigate. I gave them no information, subjugated my wants, and expressed only positive feelings. This left them to make their own assumptions, and human nature suspects the worst.

No wonder I sought solace on trails. As a child, I'd jumped on a bus when getting away, trapping me on the route it was following and forcing me off at the end of the line. As an adult, I discovered I had more control when using my own feet, reinforcing the belief I could only count on myself to get me where I was going.

What peace I found out in the wild was a temporary truce, it never lasted. I had mastered enduring, hanging on without purpose or ending. It kept me going, but it wasn't the solution. If I was going to change, I needed to move toward endurance, where actions had intent and a finish line, and the strength I'd built was an asset. To stop running away from everything and start running toward something.

Dry mouth pulled me from introspection. Looking ahead, I spotted a trail with tiny runners climbing a distant mountain's flank. There, the next aid station waited, likely three miles away.

I'd taken my last sip of water almost half an hour ago, already parched and feeling the physical effects. Three miles uphill in the afternoon heat was not a good proposition. Still, stopping wouldn't get me there faster, so I trudged on. Thoughts quieted as discomfort and fear took over.

Cresting a small hill, I glimpsed heaven. Ahead, in the middle of this barren land, stood a small oasis with several trees. A mirage? As I got closer, I could see there was a cold spring bubbling up from the ground.

I splashed it on my face and head, filled my bottle, drank it empty, then filled it again. The water tasted clean and pure. As cold water descended my throat, I imagined a glacier sliding down my body and felt instant refreshment. I wet my trusty bandana, placing it around my neck to help cool me down further. Then I drenched my hat, letting the cold water run down my face through dried, salty sweat. It cleared the darker thoughts from my head, refilling my optimism. I continued along the trail filled with gratitude for that little oasis that had turned my day around.

The heat quickly sucked up all the moisture. In less than a mile, everything was completely dry, and I was hot again. I'd make it to the next aid station, but then it was three miles back down before continuing through the blast zone several more miles. I wasn't sure I could survive another round of this burning desolation.

7

I stumbled into the Windy Ridge aid station at 4:51 PM with thirty miles behind me. The oasis had revived me, but the past eighteen hot, dry miles were taking a toll. With long races, I liked to count mileage completed, rather than what was left. If I had concentrated on the 176 miles remaining, it would have felt like a prison sentence. Fifteen percent down, on the other hand, felt good. It was subtle, yet it made a huge difference. I used this strategy in my personal life as well. I didn't think about what was left to do, instead trying to stay in the moment and think about what I'd accomplished.

This was a "no crew" location, meaning runners and volunteers only. I worked through my checklist alone. Top off the water, chug some down. I wasn't eating and nothing else needed attention, so I was quickly back on the trail. It was difficult for me to eat solids when running, add high heat, like I'd been experiencing, and my body had zero desire for food. Exercise shunts blood flow away from the digestive tract, so I wasn't unique in low appetite, having to force calories in. I relied mostly on gels and liquids to feed my body.

The four-mile easy descent ahead was a gift, a fairly straight fire road back down into the blast zone. Waiting at the bottom was a long, steady climb full of rolling hills to the next aid station 9.6 miles away, with 1,552 feet down and 1,703 feet going up. The air felt slightly cooler, I had made it past the peak of the day's heat.

From here, I had a clear view of the destruction. The 1980 eruption had stripped this side of the mountain down to bedrock and ash, leaving behind what geologists cheerfully term a "debris avalanche deposit." The pyroclastic flow had traveled at 300 mph, turning old-growth forest into matchsticks in seconds, leaving behind what now, thirty-seven years later, still resembled a moonscape.

With few hazards to worry about, my mind went blissfully quiet. I'd gotten through the worst the beginning of the race had to offer, and for the moment, there were few concerns. My body had slipped into conservation mode, recognizing even thinking was taking up valuable resources. Running just happened, like breathing. It felt like my natural state, as basic as lying in bed. I knew this feeling wouldn't last. These moments would come and go, which was all the more reason to appreciate them.

Mount Saint Helens loomed in front of me, in all her glory, owning the landscape. I could see where the eruption had torn away a huge portion of this side in its geological tantrum. Gray rocks left a massive, barren scar that went for several miles, bordered by green trees. Her top was dusted with white, the last of the season's snow hanging on. The lesser peaks of the Cascade Range surrounded it. I felt grateful for this extraordinary view and the brief distraction it provided.

As I descended from this out-and-back jaunt to the aid station, I saw the young, early twenty-something woman from earlier in the race making her way up. She was singing with a dance to her step as she power-walked up the hill. I was jealous of her energy, but at this pace, she'd be flirting with cutoff times. The dancing and singing burned valuable energy, I worried she might exhaust herself. Yet it was obvious she was happy, and it wasn't my problem, so there was nothing to be done. We exchanged a smile as we passed each other.

The temperature had dipped a bit into the eighties. As I reached the bottom of the fire road and turned onto the single-track, rocks started jutting across the trail, so my focus returned to my steps. The terrain was uneven as I worked my way up. Sometimes I would have to take a large step, a couple feet high, other times a small one, just a few inches. I had plenty of water and was drinking often, but couldn't seem to slake my thirst.

Right on time, my anxiety trickled in, but this time, as it pushed me to go faster, I forced myself to slow down in an attempt to bypass my neurotic loop of speed begetting worry begetting breathlessness begetting more worry. The experiment seemed to be working.

Pondering the anxiety and suffering running seemed to bring, I returned to the unanswered question that had been dogging me now for months.

Why am I doing this?

Of course, there were the default answers. The health benefits. The sense of accomplishment and carrying that over into my life. It helped balance my mental health. I would often joke that I was here because I had an open weekend with nothing else to do. There was the adventure of it all.

Blah, blah, blah.

Those were the easy answers. They satisfied anyone who asked, but they were superficial. Yet I knew there was something more, under the surface. Why was I doing this to myself?

The question arrived with the harder truth bubbling up behind it. I was running off anxiety, burning the extra energy so it didn't build up and explode like the volcano I was traversing. I was running to make myself so tired that I didn't have to deal with stress. It was a method of managing my anxiety without dealing with it. Letting off enough steam that the engine didn't blow without fixing the problem causing the buildup. While my mind grasped onto a sense of peace during long runs, it wasn't a solution, instead a temporary patch I had to keep reapplying.

As I pushed forward, evidence of life was slowly returning to the trail. A bush here, a small tree there. A patch of green grass, maybe even a single flower. I passed by, barely noticing as my thoughts churned.

I run to escape.

The answer popped into my head. I wanted to reject it as untrue, but I couldn't. I ran these long distances to get away from reality and rationalize the situation until I could accept it. It kept me going and allowed bouts of happiness, but I knew it was unsustainable. By rationalizing problems, I could put on a great front and appear strong and capable. It fooled many people, myself included. It was like woodworking, I thought, thinking of my workshop. It is often difficult to see the weak points in a piece of wood until it breaks. I appeared strong, but I knew there were cracks inside that needed attention.

"Dude!"

I looked up, taken by surprise. I had arrived at the Johnston Observatory aid station, oblivious to my surroundings. The deep voice was definitely not Jenni, and I didn't know anyone else out here. I looked up, confused, and there he was, grinning widely at me.

"Dude!" I hollered back happily, the extra weight I'd been carrying in my mind evaporating instantly.

It was the aid station worker who'd dosed me with purple electrolytes at the Blue Lake stop. It felt good to be recognized. He put up a hand, and I high-fived without hesitation.

"Whatcha need?" he asked as Jenni was approaching.

"Water, please?"

He grabbed the pack I had taken off and stepped away to refill it.

Jenni and I hugged, had a quick kiss, and then she asked the inevitable question. "Have you eaten?"

"No, but you know me."

"Well, you should eat something soon."

I knew she was worried and probably right, but my body wasn't ready. It would be a mistake.

"How about some electrolytes?" I asked as a compromise.

I knew the electrolytes would make her happy, and they came in a sugary beverage that would load calories in. She ran off to grab some as the aid station worker returned.

"I didn't expect to see you here," I said as I started digging through my pack.

"I'm jumping from one station to another for the whole race."

"Nice! So, I'll get to see you again?"

"If the timing works!" he said enthusiastically.

"What's your name?"

"Dave."

"Well, I hope I see you again, Dave!"

"Me too, 35!" he said, referencing my race bib number, before heading off to help another runner coming in behind me.

Jenni reappeared as I pulled my light jacket and headlamp out of the pack. It was 8:52 PM, and the sun was going down. I'd need light soon, and weather reports said it would get cold tonight. I wanted these close so I didn't have to take my pack off to get them later. I stuffed them into front pockets, the ultra-runner's equivalent of loading magazines before battle, then threw on my pack while Jenni waited patiently with the drink. I chugged it down, and with one more quick kiss, I was on my way.

Many runners like to take their time in aid stations, sit down if they can, and rest a bit. I preferred to move through them quickly. It saved time to compensate for my slow running, but mostly because I'm afraid that if I get too relaxed, I won't want to keep going.

Leaving Johnston Observatory, I got one last look at Helen, as I was calling her now, dropping all formalities. We'd been through so much together by this point, I felt confident she was good with this. Helen looked beautiful, reflecting the orange light of sunset. It had been a tough day, yet I survived.

6.6 miles to the next aid station, a route that was almost all downhill or flat, possibly the easiest leg of the entire race. The trail led down the back of Mount Margaret, obscuring Helen. I was pretty sure I would not see her again, so I took a moment to silently thank her as she slipped out of sight. Ahead was 2,264 feet of easy down and only 574 feet of elevation gain. As the sun went down, the temperature was dropping fast.

Going up the front side of Helen at the start was green and lush. The back side brought the desert heat and moonscapes. Now, further away, I could see different effects from the volcano blast. There were still thousands of dead trees, their huge trunks devoid of branches as they lay lined up in a perfect row where they'd fallen forty years ago, a landscape littered with the skeletons of a forest long since passed. They reminded me of bleached, bare cattle bones in the desert. A graveyard for titans, with new life hesitant to come into this sacred ground.

As darkness fell, my mind turned inward, musing on the way towering giants could be toppled by an unexpected blast. I could be toppled too. I was attempting a 200-mile run, yet carried the shame of my heart condition. The stents had resulted in nightly pharmaceutical surrender. A statin to keep my cholesterol low, and a baby aspirin to keep my blood from clotting around the stents. The medications felt like punishment for not being better. I wanted family and friends to forget about my heart, but I never did.

I hadn't told Jenni that I was taking meds until I could no longer sneak them. When I finally did, it felt like confessing a sin. Of course, she didn't care, but I remained discreet afterward. I didn't discuss heart issues with my family either, except when necessary, as a cautionary tale. I'd told my siblings because I wanted them to be aware of the genetic risks. Maybe it would encourage them to make healthier choices and live longer. When it came to me, however, I would only engage in talk about health if it involved how far I could push my body. It didn't seem to matter how far I ran, I couldn't outrun the shame I felt.

The irony wasn't lost on me. Here I was, running myself into the ground to prove I wasn't broken, when needing to prove anything suggested I was.

Now in darkness, I saw the headlamp of another runner in the distance ahead of me, reminding me of one of my personal tenets of night trail-running: wait until absolutely necessary for the headlamp because batteries are limited. Even though it should carry enough charge to get me through the night, and I carried a spare, I still worried I would end up running in the dark. Jenni would be changing out and recharging the batteries for me between nights, but it was still a concern.

As often happened, I'd waited too long as a result of my caution. There was moonlight, yet it would be easy to miss a tripping hazard in the dimness. I reached up, turned it on, and for the last two miles I gladly followed the forward-facing beam.

Arriving at the Coldwater Lake aid station at 11:03 PM, I found Jenni waiting exactly where the trail emerged, her warm eyes lighting up when she saw me. She had been amazing support so far, ready and present at each aid station, taking care of me with zero criticism and solid suggestions. This race felt like the early days of our relationship, when we were teammates working toward the same goals.

Over time, the relationship felt more like I was the clay, and she was the sculptor shaping me into what she wanted. Instead of talking about my feelings, I began to resist until saying "no" became instinct. The race was pulling us closer again, offering hope.

This was the first aid station with sleeping options, but I wasn't stopping. Too much adrenaline coursing through my blood, and only 46.5 miles into the race. They had been tough, slow miles, but my body was used to going longer.

"Are you going to sleep?" Jenni asked, as if reading my mind.

"No, I'm good," I responded.

As soon as the words left my mouth, I recognized my standard response to everything, regardless of how I felt. I could see her hesitation, a legitimate reaction since she knew "I'm good" wasn't always my truth.

"I'm hungry, is there food?" I asked, knowing this would distract her and avoid deeper inquiry on sleep.

"Yes!" she said, digging into the bag she carried.

She held out a few options, and I grabbed the bag of trail mix. The nuts and dried fruits with chocolate candies would be a good energy boost. I also grabbed a protein bar and slid it into the front pocket of my pack.

"What else do you need?" she asked.

"That last section was easy and much cooler, so I'm fine on water. I have my headlamp, and my jacket is right here if I need it."

The high heat, aided and abetted by the desert blast zone, was relenting. The night temps were now in the sixties, much more reasonable. Faint hints of smoke from distant forest fires remained, a slight irritant but not hindering.

"You want to sit down for a minute or anything?" Jenni asked.

"Nah, I'm ready to keep going."

I saw the hesitancy again, but then I saw her decide to trust me as she shook it off without saying anything. I was again appreciative of this change, I didn't need to debate with her in this moment. It was 18.7 miles to the next aid station, and I felt confident I had everything I needed to get there.

Instead of searing desert, this section went through shaded forest at night. I wasn't going to run out of water or overheat. I had eaten a couple handfuls of trail mix and had the protein bar in my pocket.

I moved back onto the trail, running smoothly as I contemplated what was ahead. This was one of the tougher sections that went through proper Pacific Northwest forest. Western hemlock, Douglas fir, and noble fir sheltering sky, though it would be too dark to see much.

This leg started with an easy four miles of small rollers along the lake. Perfect to relax and settle into a rhythm. The cooler temperature would make the following eight miles of uphill much easier. After that, it was five miles or so back down. There would be 4,911 feet of elevation gain, with 3,740 feet of decline. Along the lake, up the mountain, down the mountain.

Unwrapping my meager protein bar, I thought of my racing friend, John, who would have his crew waiting with a huge cheeseburger, down it, then run straight up a hill in the heat. Not me. If I tried even a few bites, I'd heave it back up. The protein bar felt like a small risk, but worth it.

I stole a glance sideways and immediately regretted it as the headlamp reflected off several pairs of mammal eyes watching me pass. Lining the trail would be raccoons, rabbits, and other harmless creatures. My imagination turned them into lions and bears. When running at night, I'd learned to look straight ahead while making occasional noise. A scuffed shoe, maybe a kicked rock. Most animals want nothing to do with humans. I gave them every opportunity to go the other way.

Stop thinking about night creatures.

My thoughts returned to Jenni. We'd had a great month or so, and we felt on the same page again. In the beginning, we were inseparable. I remembered the good times but struggled to pinpoint the transition. They had been gradual changes. Small words, shadows of doubt. Just as I'd tread over bigger and bigger patches of snow that fateful training day, the danger growing with each step, our relationship was getting increasingly untenable.

Jenni confessed to me once that she felt her mom had been very critical of her while growing up. They fought over what clothes she would wear to school. How much make-up she put on. Who she dated. Too much weight gained or lost. This had been all Jenni knew. In response, she'd tried to make her mom happy, and to fit in with the popular kids at school. Being someone people liked became important to her, acceptance was how she learned to live in her world.

She likely believed she was helping me, each correction a form of guidance learned from her mother's or peers' critical scrutiny, yet they eroded my confidence, making me feel smaller. I needed approval and collapsed without it. Sensing my weakening confidence, she came harder in her attempt to bring me back. A vicious cycle where she tried fixing things that weren't broken while I denied anything needed fixing at all. We each carried past adapted behaviors into the relationship, trying to pretend they weren't there.

My headlamp reflected off a sign indicating the first out-and-back to a mountain peak. As if 200 miles weren't enough, the race director designed the course to visit every nearby summit, adding additional miles. She called it a 200-mile race, but it was actually 206.5 miles. It felt mildly sadistic.

Had I arrived during the day, I might have appreciated the jaunt, but at night, there was no rewarding view. I was climbing up to climb down. At the top, I looked to the stars for some consolation before heading back. At least it was downhill for several miles with temps now in the low fifties, perfect conditions for running.

My relationship with Jenni was the best I'd had. Between the hard moments, there was a lot of fun, love, and kindness. Maybe I was blowing things out of proportion.

You're doing it again.

Right back to finding peace where I was, creating happiness in my current situation, because I was too chicken to face the challenge. I knew deep down that if we were going to make it, then we had to work on our communication and repair our coping mechanisms. I didn't think I could continue as we were.

Whoa!

That was a revelation. I don't think I'd admitted that before, even to myself. If I were honest about my future, this wasn't what I wanted. These ancient patterns led to the same old places they always had, convincing myself to find reasons to make the present sufferably survivable.

This forced me to admit I had no plan, no goal, no direction. I was drifting in the vast ocean without a vision, waiting for things to improve. As if I would simply happen upon some Caribbean paradise if I waited long enough. Like winning the lottery as a retirement plan, this was not a good strategy. I was going to need to come up with something better.

Would Jenni make these changes with me? If not, could I leave?

I had the questions, but still wasn't ready for the answers.

Entering the crew-less Norway Pass aid station at 4:46 AM Saturday morning with this weight, I was grateful for space after the revelation. I quickly went through the aid station checklist, making a mental note to drink more in the cooler temps. Even in the cold, it was possible to dehydrate from sweating.

From here, there were 11.1 miles over large hills, with 2,339 feet uphill and 1,942 feet down, to the next aid station, where my first pacer, Kim, would be waiting. I looked forward to company after so much solitude, though I wished Joy could have made it. Kim was a good friend, but having my daughter would have been special.

Joy and I had run together often before she left for college. We would jog slowly along as we talked, catching up on everything happening in our worlds. One time, late into a longer jaunt and struggling up a steep hill, she found herself fumbling, not finding what she wanted to say. After starting and stopping a few times, she finally blurted out in frustration, "Words are hard!"

We both had a good laugh over that and still used that phrase when unable to get out what we wanted to express.

Still, I knew she was with me in spirit. Without her encouragement, I wouldn't be here. I would have walked away after that devastating weekend. She was following my pattern by being the caring, supportive one for others, while quietly hoping someone would be there for her too. I tried to be, but feared I failed at it too often.

But is she supporting you, or the illusion of you?

I'd worked hard to be the strong, stable father I thought they needed. Did she believe the lie I'd created? Would she still support the man running scared and anxious? Same with my son, Chris. Was he proud of me, or the person I wanted him to think I was? It was a frightening possibility that my kids might love the character on the stage, not the actor playing the role.

If it's true with your kids, it's probably true with everyone else.

Like my mom. My brothers and sisters. My friends. Especially Jenni. I gave them someone to love, but I didn't know how much of it was me. I wondered if the real me was lovable, if they all would still be here if they knew the man petrified with fear inside. My body shook with the idea. I let it keep shaking, trying to get the feeling to go away. I needed to let go of these thoughts driving me downward.

As a distraction, I reflected on the Trail Runner Nation podcast that had introduced me to the Bigfoot 200. More than once, they discussed early morning running as "free miles," when time passed quietly and simply. The body and mind were tired as numb miles passed unnoticed, with seemingly little effort. When the sun came up, the mind and body would wake, as if those miles had never happened. That's why they referred to them as "free."

As advertised, the next few miles passed quietly and uneventfully. Unconscious running as light broke over the eastern mountains. If I'd been meditating, this would easily have been empty mind.

I breathed in deep gratitude as the sun broke over the dark, shaded mountaintops. There's magic in the sunrise, my favorite part of early morning runs. Few people take time to enjoy sunrises, especially in the middle of nowhere.

I was now about seventy-five miles in, so as I ran into Elk Pass aid station at 10:53 AM, hugging Jenni and Kim, I prepared to attempt a nap.

"Are you okay if I try and sleep, Kim?" I asked, worried because she'd traveled all the way here, waited for me to arrive, and now I was asking her to wait while I snoozed.

Crazy runner, endless waiting.

"Yup!" she responded.

The volunteers directed me to a tent with a firm cot and a woolly, itchy blanket. After thanking them, I laid down for the first time in over twenty-four hours. I wanted to fall asleep, but doubt harassed me.

With 130 miles to go, did I have what it takes?

8

The tent was like a sauna designed by sadomasochists. Hard cot, rough itchy covers, late morning sun bearing down and baking me inside. I lay there overhearing Jenni and Kim talking in the distance. While they were not close, they had become fast friends as soon as they met. It had been a few months since they last saw each other, so while I could not hear what they were saying, I was certain they were catching up on life events.

The volunteers were at their station about fifty feet away, chatting. I could hear runners as they came and went, moving on as I lay there. None of it was enough to be distracting, yet I couldn't relax. Sleep wouldn't come.

At least my body was resting, I justified, glancing at my watch. It had only been fifteen minutes. I'd planned on a forty-five-minute nap, so I forced myself to remain. The heat was intense, sweat glistening on my skin. After thirty minutes, I decided it had been a mistake to try and sleep. As tired as I was, it wasn't going to be.

I crawled out of the tent to find Kim.

"You good to go?" I asked.

"Sure!" she replied, full of energy.

Jenni had refilled my water, stuffed a new protein bar in my pack, and thrown out the garbage. "Perfect, thank you!" I appreciated her.

"You should eat more," Jenni said.

I wanted to refuse, but things were going very well between us. If eating a protein bar kept it that way, then I'd eat ten.

"Toss me a bar, please."

I ate it right there so she could see I was serious. I could not do most protein bars, finding them chalky or flavorless, so I had taken to Clif Builder bars. I really liked the mint chocolate ones and bought them by the box. Jenni referred to them as "candy bars" because they were sweet and full of sugar. She wasn't wrong. Still, I would willingly eat them, and they provided protein and energy, so they became my go-to. A quick kiss with Jenni, and then Kim and I hit the road.

As the aid station disappeared behind trees, I realized I hadn't yet checked in with Jenni to see how she was doing. I had been wrapped up in my experience, solely focused on pushing forward. There weren't any obvious signs I could recall that she was having a hard time, but she wouldn't want me to see if there were. It worked both ways.

She was working diligently between aid stations to support me, and I was failing to acknowledge it. I made a mental note to check in with her at the next stop.

I was surprised my brain wasn't foggy yet, I was still thinking clearly. I recalled what I knew of the stretch ahead. Fifteen miles to the next aid station. Long climbs were gone for the moment, this was going to be a lot of mountainous, upward rolling hills to achieve the 2,759 feet to the top. Then followed a long descent, where I'd finish with 3,343 feet down. There would be plenty of tree cover to keep the heat off, which was nice after the hot tent. This leg had the highest altitude so far, it could potentially affect my breathing.

I slowed to a fast hike to start, partly from fatigue, partly to enjoy Kim's company. One steep climb followed another. We would jog the downhills, but they felt very short compared to the ascents. I felt less rushed, more peaceful, as if I was just out on a run with a friend. We stopped for pictures at a spectacular vista.

Anxiety had driven yesterday's push, trying to stay ahead of the dark thoughts. There is a plus side to anxiety, it propelled me to accomplish great things. It also ate away at me constantly, wearing me down. I hadn't known I had anxiety until recently. To me, it was something other people had.

I didn't have panic attacks, rapid heartbeats, or a sense of dread, but a friend's description of social anxiety hit home. We were discussing an upcoming friend's baby shower.

"I don't know if I'm going to go," she said.

"Why not? It will be fun!" I countered, even though I wasn't sure I was going either.

"I get stressed out in crowds of people. I'm a bit nervous," she replied.

"Really? I wouldn't have known that." She seemed very social to me.

"Yeah, I have anxiety, though most people wouldn't know. I've started avoiding things that really stress me out to help. I used to force myself to go to parties like this, or hang out with friends, and I always dreaded it. I would be nervous the whole time, feeling restless."

I knew exactly what she was talking about, except I usually skipped the party altogether. I didn't like the nervous, stressed, restless feelings. Could I have it too?

"Yeah, looking back, I can see how it affected me," she continued. "Remember when I was in theater?"

"Yeah, everyone does, you were great!" We'd all thought she would end up on Broadway or in Hollywood someday.

"I started turning down roles cause I was a nervous wreck. I turned down a lot of other opportunities too. When I could barely hold a job as a barista, I finally started looking for some help. I'm doing much better now. I think I may even start acting again. Not sure I'm ready to be stuck in a crowded house with a bunch of other people though," she finished.

I'd walked away from job promotions, travel opportunities, and relationships because of similar fears without recognizing the pattern. In truth, I had been letting anxiety manage my life. A lot of things made sense through this lens, including my need to be out on the trail.

Kim proved to be an excellent pacer, knowing when to push, slow down, talk, or stay silent. We'd met through Beth's running group and became friends quickly with her fun and light personality. She was a lean, tall Asian woman who had always been much faster than the slower group I ran with, yet she enjoyed our company. To challenge herself, she would often run ahead, then circle back to join us for a bit of conversation before taking off again, literally running circles around us. She could see me retreating inward and let me be as we moved in silence.

I briefly wondered how I was doing in the race. I knew better than to think I might be toward the front of the pack. Running taught me humility quickly. During one of my first races, I started to feel a little confident, maybe even cocky, about how well things were going. Less than a minute later, a heavyset woman in her sixties whizzed by me. I started running faster, trying to pass her, but it didn't take long before I had to admit I couldn't keep up. I slowed down while she continued off into the distance, finishing long before me.

Gender, age, and body type said nothing about a person's ability. The longer the distance, the more equality between runners. Women have incredible endurance in comparison to the male proclivity for speed and strength. Age and wisdom tended to pace better than the speed and energy of youth. No one would guess I had several stents in my heart, nor would I have guessed this woman could outrun me by so much. Trying to match someone else's pace, to run their race instead of my own, was never a recipe for success. I cleared other runners from my head, letting that stressor go.

My mind was getting a little foggy around the edges, and thoughts were coming slower. Fatigue brought memories of mile seventy-eight during my first hundred-mile race, about the distance I was at now. I'd been running alone in the dark for several hours, feeling mentally and physically exhausted. When my body started to shiver uncontrollably from the cold, I decided to quit at the next aid station, imagining getting into the warm car and heading back to the hotel where there was food, a hot shower, and a soft bed waiting.

The last half mile to the aid station was downhill, so I started running faster. With smiling crew waiting there to support me, I soon had food in my stomach and a warm, dry running jacket. I refilled my water as we joked, and before I knew it, I was back out on the trail.

After running a mile or two, the excitement of the aid station started to wear off, and I remembered I was supposed to quit. The plan was to be at the hotel by now, yet here I was back out in the cold and dark. Caught up in the energy of the aid station, I had forgotten how bad things were just minutes before. I realized I either had to keep going for fifteen more miles or turn around and go back, but my people would no longer be there.

I pressed on, never thought about quitting again, and finished the race. Because I couldn't quit when I wanted to, I was able to go another twenty-two miles to the finish.

Pausing at the peak for another gorgeous vista, I sensed beauty but couldn't feel it, as if seeing a picture rather than experiencing it. Starting downhill, the brain fog lifted, and I unearthed a second wind, or perhaps twentieth wind by now, and with it some clarity and energy. Kim and I started up conversation again, exchanging past running stories. She shared a time running a race with her dog that had been a series of starts and stops as he surged ahead, then stopped to sniff and mark his territory before sprinting ahead again.

I shared a race story when I joined several runners following a person who had just been out for a jog, only realizing we were well off course when we arrived at their home. Kim and I laughed, and before we knew it, the next aid station suddenly materialized before us.

This aid station was simply called Road 9327, so remote Jenni could only locate it with GPS coordinates. All the other aid stations were named after the campsite, parking lot, trailhead, or recreation area that housed them. There, they could bring in large trucks full of equipment, tents, food, and everything else needed to set up a full-service stop. Here, however, there was nothing around but the nameless road that the trail intersected and the scarce resources the volunteers had been able to haul in.

I was ninety-one miles into the race at 7:16 PM, staring down the halfway point on the early side of the time window I had predicted arriving. I thanked Kim for joining me, her welcome company had helped those miles go by with less worry and pain. I suffered another protein bar while an aid station volunteer refilled my water for me.

"How you doing?" I asked Jenni, taking advantage of the moment to check on her finally.

"I'm doing good," she answered enthusiastically.

"Are you eating and drinking water?" I asked, knowing it would be easy for her to neglect herself while taking care of me.

"I am. Promise," she said appreciatively. "How are you doing?"

"Much better than I thought I'd be at this point."

"That's amazing. I don't know how you do it," she said, looking at me with admiration.

"I don't know how either," I joked, shrugging off the compliment as usual.

Maybe she complimented me more than I recognized. With my tendency to dismiss positives and own negatives, the balance seemed skewed. Something to add to my long list of insights to be explored. Later.

After stalling several minutes, unusual for my quick transitions, I said goodbyes and headed out alone. The sluggish stop was further evidence fatigue was settling in, evicting any feeling of urgency. I sensed the light waning, though it was subtle because the prolific trees and mountains seemed to keep everything in constant shadow.

My brain was sluggish yet still functioning as it retrieved the information I was looking for. This section was twenty-one miles long with 4,272 miles of elevation gain and 5,886 decline, a tough one. As I moved down the trail, my quads were voicing dissent with hints of mutiny while the sadness of renewed isolation settled in. Even the silent miles with Kim felt better from just having another presence. I was grateful the rest of my crew would start joining me at the next stop.

My mom was flying out to support me from the sidelines. I was surprised when she asked if she could come help, responding with "Of course! I don't care how old you are, it's always great when Mom comes to your game!"

This was very true, at least for me. As one of eight kids with a single mom, I'd only participated in after-school sports that were free and did not require her to transport me anywhere. She was always working or taking care of someone else, so it was extremely rare for her to attend a game. I was sadly left to manage myself, as I still did to this day.

It wasn't my mom's fault, she was doing the absolute best she could with what little she had to work with. Yet at the time, the young boy was left wondering if she even wanted to be at my events, we never discussed it. A part of me hoped she did, the rest feared she was grateful for the excuse to not be there. I never asked because I didn't want her to feel guilty, though perhaps more so because I was afraid of the answer.

In a way, her flying out here answered whether she'd wanted to attend my events growing up. Yet I still worried, was she proud of me or the mask I'd worn so long?

Just keep moving forward. Stay in the moment. Focus on what's in front of you.

These strategies got me through rough times, but weren't working in the big picture. Because of them, I endured to survive another day, but I wasn't building toward anything.

The second day's sun was going down quickly, the mountains hiding it long before it would dip below the ocean somewhere off to the west, and I felt true cold for the first time since the start line. I stopped briefly to put my jacket on, followed by the headlamp, lit yet again at the last moment.

Eyes forward, I reminded myself only to look immediately to each side. The retinas of night creatures reflected back at me, creeping me out. Was the great horned owl hooting a friendly hello, or warning me those were cougar eyes glaring green at me? I looked directly in front of me, allowing no deviation.

Light rain began, igniting my greatest worry of being cold and wet simultaneously. It was a bad combination that sapped energy quickly and left me miserable every time. Fortunately, for the moment, it remained a light drizzle without a noticeable temperature drop, so the light jacket was keeping up.

I flashed back to the joy of a run from a few years ago in a California forest as rain poured down. The memory brought back the child-like feeling of splashing through large mud puddles, sending water flying that I'd relived on that day. I had finished the run, soaked to the bone, gleeful.

Increasing raindrops now had me laughing out loud, enjoying the moment. I wasn't going to let a little water stop me, now determined to enjoy it. The rain continued over the next couple of hours, and thankfully, the cold continued holding off.

The drizzle was pure Pacific Northwest, marine air mass hitting the Cascades, dropping moisture to feed the temperate rainforest. It felt cleansing, washing away the lingering wildfire smoke and filling the air with petrichor. A favorite word I used when I could for the distinct, earthy, and pleasant scent that comes from fresh rain.

I had slowed down, the chased feeling dissipating. Yesterday's pushing came from all the anxiety-ridden things that kept me moving, including Jenni. It had become difficult to relax when I pondered our relationship, fearing another hammer would fall.

Each time I played the part of the nail, providing little resistance. Like the time a good artist friend gifted me her painting, which was not my usual style. Nevertheless, I appreciated the beauty and hung it up. The next time Jenni was over at my house, she paused in front of it for a moment before declaring with full authority, "That's ugly, take it down."

I wanted to explain where it came from and why I liked it, but there was no opportunity. She had handed down judgment. No questions, no curiosity, no grace for alternate opinions.

I was tempted to challenge her, but I knew it wouldn't do any good. She was unlikely to change her mind, so I took it down and avoided the battle I knew I would lose, inciting conflict within myself instead.

The trails, however, were a judgment-free zone. Tonight, it was just me, the rain, the trees, and the glowing eyes in the brush. I could find peace despite my damp clothes. I didn't even worry about potential chafing.

As the rain eased and I ran on through the night, I pondered how I had committed to this 200-mile adventure. I had committed to big vacations, difficult jobs. I spent eighteen months later in life finishing off my bachelor's degree.

Why am I so willing to commit to these things, then hold back on moving in with Jenni?

Within a breath, I had answered myself.

You know why.

As the rain stopped and the moon peeked out from the clouds, I knew I was not avoiding commitment. I was avoiding the big questions required to get to the truth of who we were together. I needed to have the crucial discussions with Jenni I avoided because I was scared of the answers. Even more scared of taking action if they didn't align with what I wanted. Yet if we worked everything out, conquering the disruptors in our relationship, I would be excited to move in together.

It was past midnight, and the trail leveled into small rolling hills. I could hear a river rushing along next to me, but I couldn't see it, even with the headlamp. This river was evidence I was early in the last six miles of this segment. I hadn't slept in over forty hours. I was finally starting to feel hungry. Yet the trail just kept going. And going.

The sound of water rushing over rocks didn't change. The small hills went up and down with negligible variation. The headlamp exposed nothing but an invariable muddy path bordered by brush. I was on an endless treadmill, making no progress. Time had stopped moving, monotony enveloped me, and inevitably, I began to dwell on Jenni again.

Like me, she wanted to belong, to be accepted. I believed her criticisms were her way of trying to help me, to mold me into her version of a more likable person. Being someone people liked was how she had learned to exist in the world. Now she was just trying to keep it all from falling apart, including me.

The way she treated me was likely her way of caring for me. She looked after me and protected me from perceived worse judgment from outsiders. If I wore the right clothes, if I had the right art on my walls, if I liked the right wines, then people would like me. When she was most critical, she was, in her own way, showing me love. She wanted to be liked, and so it was important for people to like me too. For them to like us as a couple. The problem was that her way of loving and protecting wasn't working for me. I was holding onto it all.

Like the trail before me, my relationship felt dark, muddy, and endless. I prided myself on endurance, but this wasn't constructive. True endurance was what I was doing in this race. It had a purpose, a goal. I had to put in the work, and there was a finish line, after which it would be over. The reward was completing the task and feeling good about what I had accomplished.

Enduring, on the other hand, was what I was doing in my relationship. Hanging on, running on a treadmill until collapse. Like this endless footpath before me. I broke through the trees and into the Lewis River aid station just as my mind inquired.

How much longer can you go?

I wasn't certain if I was talking about the race or the relationship.

9

It was dark at 4:46 AM Sunday morning, but I recognized the Lewis River aid station right away. This had been the scene of my training weekend catastrophe. Multiple cold river crossings, the insole folding over, and the beginning of the doubt that led me to quit the following day. The geography of failure, etched fast in my memory.

"Dad!"

Chris appeared with Jenni, running to meet me. He'd be pacing me for this section, the one I dreaded most. We embraced tightly, and I gave Jenni a big hug despite my barnyard aroma. She handed me water, exactly what I needed.

"Are you hungry?" she asked hopefully.

"Sleep," was all I managed. When her face fell, I continued, "Then food. Hungry. But now sleep."

I sounded like a caveman, but it was the best I could do at the moment.

"Over here," she said, guiding me behind the busy volunteer area to several tents.

A volunteer recorded my request to wake up in one hour, then assigned me to one of the small tents. I'd been spoiled at the last aid station with a cot. This location offered only a thin pad and a wool blanket. I lay down for only the second time in almost forty-eight hours.

Despite exhaustion, sleep didn't come immediately. The blanket felt soft and luxurious in comparison to the previous scratchy one, though that might have been delirium. Fear crept in. Would it be a repeat of last time?

When I'd recommitted myself to start the Bigfoot 200, reaching Lewis River at 112.5 miles had been the goal. Farther than I'd ever run before. I was here, I'd made it. Something to be proud of.

What will they think if I quit?

I rolled over, trying to get comfortable and quiet my mind.

Only my daughter knew about my previous failure, a secret I'd guarded these past five weeks. What would Chris think if I told him I was done, that we weren't running together? What would Jenni say? Clearly, my constant companion of potential disappointment had also managed to survive the distance.

Despite the difficulty of the last several miles, I wasn't ready to quit. I felt like I had more in me. Fortunately, I didn't have to decide now, I'd deal with that when I woke up. With the release came sleep, hard and fast.

The volunteer's wake-up call felt like only five minutes, but a watch check proved the hour. Unlike normal mornings of lazy puttering about, I got right up and moving. My mind knew there was work to be done.

Searching for Jenni and Chris, my body felt marginally refreshed. The sunrise helped, as did deep breaths of the clean morning air. Not rested by any means, but more energy and easier movement. I found them, knowing what I was going to ask, but I didn't like it.

"Where's the bathroom?" I inquired.

I'd secretly hoped to avoid this logistical nightmare, rationalizing that minimal eating plus constant movement would bypass the need entirely. The body had other plans. They pointed the way, but I hesitated.

"Do you have my stuff?" I asked Jenni

She pointed to a wagon full of labeled plastic tubs. Food, spare equipment, clothes, and shoes. I had the idea that if I was "dropping trou," I might as well change my clothes. Jenni pulled out a full wardrobe change and passed it over.

With my hands full, I headed off in the indicated direction.

The campground bathrooms consisted of a cinder block building housing two small rooms with large plastic toilets, essentially white tubes with seats over giant latrine holes. More posh than a porta-potty, but not by much.

Better than squatting in the woods.

I sat slowly, aching muscles protesting. Time blurred, I had no concept of its passing. I might have dozed or simply stared into space. I could have been there minutes or hours. A knock on the door brought me back to consciousness.

"Occupied," I shouted, noting from overheard conversation that a line had formed outside.

I needed to get moving, if for no other reason than to not delay others. Changing clothes became an unexpectedly complex project. Stiff, sore limbs moved reluctantly, lacking any form of grace. I nearly fell while removing my shorts, wrestling with the tight spandex replacement designed for wicking sweat and avoiding chafing. The shirt change resembled a circus act. Kneeling to tie shoes wasn't easy and required more effort than it should have to return to standing.

Exiting to dirty looks, I realized I'd monopolized the facility too long and didn't feel better in fresh clothes. Changing was likely pointless, but too late for that.

"What do you want to eat?" Jenni asked.

"A burrito?" I'd read stories online from past runners about these legendary burritos, and planned to devour several during the race.

"What do you want in it?" Chris asked.

"Everything?"

"Done!" he said, running off to get it.

"Do you need your feet taped?" Jenni asked.

"I dunno..." I was conflicted, having never had my feet taped before.

The Pacific Northwest's abundant river crossings lay ahead. The region's geology created countless stream valleys as the Cascade Range intercepted Pacific moisture, dropping it in predictable patterns that carved waterways through ancient volcanic terrain. Eventually, they converged to form the huge Columbia River that carried Lewis and Clark through the end of their journey to the Pacific Ocean.

"There's several river crossings ahead, it might prevent blisters," she said, almost pleadingly.

"Let's do it." The easy answer, plus a chance to sit down.

Jenni guided me over to where volunteers were taping people's feet. I was extremely appreciative to the race organizers for thinking of these things. Even more so for all the volunteers. Who, I wondered, gives up their weekend to work on the sweaty, stinky, gross feet of strangers?

"35!" With that shout, I had my answer.

"Dave! You're everywhere, man!" I responded happily.

"Come sit down."

As he pulled my shoes and socks off, I was glad I'd just changed them, though I knew my feet would still be gross. Medical tape stuck no matter how wet it might get in rivers, rain, or sweat. Most importantly, it protected skin from rubbing against shoes, socks, and whatever else, which over dozens of miles would sprout blisters.

Even though the tape would protect my feet from this, a general running rule is "nothing new on race day." Any number of things could happen when a new element is introduced, most of them bad, but I figured the tape was low risk and making Jenni happy equaled high reward.

As Dave went to work on my feet, Chris handed me an epic breakfast burrito filled with eggs, bacon, sausage, cheese, avocado, and more. It was far from my usual running fare, but I was hungry and dove into it immediately. It tasted every bit as good as I'd heard, maybe better. It could have been hunger, but I firmly believed that burrito would have been heaven on any day.

Sitting there, being cared for, felt good. This whole race, I'd felt supported in many ways, especially by Jenni. It reminded me of when I was more open-minded to her suggestions, before reflexive rebellion became my default.

As I devoured the burrito, I mentally reviewed the upcoming section. 18.9 miles of brutal trail that had already beaten me once. Fifteen miles of rolling uphill, totaling 5,518 feet of elevation gain, then four miles of gradual descent, totaling 3,363 feet. We'd hit soft soil, treacherous river crossings, and low oxygen due to high elevation. One of the toughest sections of the course, as I could personally attest.

I was going through the motions of leaving with Chris, but I hadn't decided yet. I wanted to, but I was also dragging my feet. I'd been here three hours already, killing time, finding new ways to avoid committing. I was scared about what was ahead, scared of failing again. I was also scared of what quitting meant. Just like in my relationship. I looked about, wondering what else I could find to delay.

"You ready to go?" Chris asked eagerly.

With nothing to save me in sight, I surrendered to my fate. Mustering as much enthusiasm as I could, I said, "Let's do this!"

"Go get 'em man!" Dave hollered, giving me a quick hug. "I'll see you later!"

"Absolutely!" I said, full of confidence I didn't have.

Off into the trees we went while Jenni packed for the drive to the next station. It was hard not to be happy around Chris. At twenty-four, working at a non-profit he loved despite better-paying options available, he was content. Slightly taller than me, with long shaggy hair, a full beard, and ice-blue eyes that looked right into you as if he saw your soul, his infectious, positive energy was exactly what I needed.

Chris was much more athletic than I had ever been, playing a variety of sports in school, skateboarding, and surfing. When Joy started running and doing races with me, his competitiveness came out, and he started running too. Though it wasn't a regular activity in his life, he kept fit through everything else he was doing. Even without training, he was still faster than me in anything less than a half-marathon. Had he taken the time to train, he would be faster than me over longer distances too.

When we visited each other, we would always make time to go running, him slowing down for me, using the opportunity to talk about everything from daily life details to delving into philosophy. It was interesting how much more open and wide-ranging conversation could be over a good run or walk. How just getting outside and doing something different changed the dynamic, opening the heart and mind. I'd found this to be true with anyone I had the opportunity to run or walk with.

Today, he was all smiles and happy to be on this adventure together, the perfect person for this section. I'd planned each of my pacers intentionally, trying to best match their availability, pace, and personality to the terrain. Knowing this section would be tough physically and mentally for me, Chris was the right fit. As we ran slowly along the trail, my body and mind were waking up.

Before I knew it, we reached the first river crossing. Five short weeks ago, this had been rushing, ice-cold, waist-deep water that required navigation across fallen trees to cross. Today, the water ran strong, but only half as deep and flowing more slowly. The shift from winter runoff to early summer had transformed my nemesis from a thirty-minute orienteering challenge to a thirty-second wading. On the other side dragons clearly marked the trail I'd had to search for previously.

We talked as we ran, catching up on his work, dating life, and friends, moving at a steady pace. It felt more like an easy weekend run than day three with less than two hours of sleep. My anxiety released as we joked and laughed. I was surprisingly alert, having expected to be a zombie by this stage.

A key difference from my previous experience here was that I was enjoying the moment. This was the third step I'd adopted from my disastrous training weekend: have fun. Last time I ran here with the jaws of the beast closing in. Today was easy and light. I had let go of the anxieties that were chasing me, of the expectations I had loaded on myself. I was living in the moment, letting joy reign, and it changed everything.

Each river crossing proved easier as we settled into a rhythm. Nine crossings total, each in water barely reaching my calves. The cold soothed tired legs rather than shocking them. I paused in each for a few seconds to let the cold do its work before continuing along the clearly marked trail, pink and orange dragons leading the way.

I was starting to think this might not be the end of my race after all. As if to test my optimism, the trail started the long climb, revealing firmer ground than expected. The soft, sliding soil had vacated the premises. No more doubling effort with each backward slip. Still steep, yet everything felt different. I was using less energy, breathing easily, and moving quickly along the trail.

As we jogged consistently upward, I thought about how awesome it was to be running with my son. A gift I was grateful for. His presence had removed all the fear out of this section. We went quiet for a bit, focused on pushing up the hill. Fond memories surfaced in the silence, including one key moment that had changed my life.

When Chris was ten, he started playing hockey. Great for me as a longtime fan of the sport. I learned to rollerblade, then ice skate, to help him train and assist with coaching.

We would practice together for hours.

One day, he asked, "Why don't you play hockey?"

Instinctively, I answered, "I can't."

"Why not?" he replied.

I always believed sincere questions deserve honest answers. If they took the time to formulate a heartfelt question, the answer should be equally thoughtful and complete. For example, when they asked about Santa with casual, child-like curiosity, I reinforced their belief. When they came to me on a quest for knowledge, I told them the facts.

Because my son had asked why I couldn't play hockey so sincerely, I reflected for a moment, only to find I didn't have an answer. There was no reason I couldn't play. My default "I can't" response was thoughtless habit. The next day, I purchased equipment and signed up for an entry-level adult hockey league.

I spent early games falling and struggling, earning the nickname "Zamboni" because I spent so much time sliding across the ice and smoothing it out. Easily the worst player, yet smiling ear to ear on the drive home, every time. Eventually, I improved, even leading the league in scoring one season.

Since then, I stopped automatically answering "I can't" to new opportunities, and my life changed. Archery class? Yes please. Yoga? Count me in! Learning to paint? Why, yes, yes I will.

In spite of our close relationship, there was no denying my need to be "super dad" affected our relationship. Did he feel pressure to appear perfect too? I was always telling my kids that it was okay to have setbacks and struggle, yet I demonstrated the opposite every day.

They had been young, nine and seven years old, when the divorce happened, yet I never showed them an ounce of hurt or struggle. One of the first things I did with my kids was take them to the zoo, where I shared how the rhinoceros got his skin and the leopard got his spots, at least according to Rudyard Kipling's book *Just So Stories*. Smiling as I explained how the rhinoceros rubbed himself up against the tree, trying to itch himself from all the cake crumbs that had gotten under his skin. All laughing as I animatedly reenacted the Ethiopian man putting spots on the leopard with his fingertips to help him hide. We stopped for ice cream I couldn't afford before dropping them off with their mom.

It was a good day, full of fond memories. Yet now I wondered what message had been delivered, never mourning my relationship with their mother in their presence. They must have wondered if I ever cared about her at all. Perhaps they wondered if I could lose them as easily.

If I had it to do over, we would still have gone to the zoo and shared the stories I had grown up with. We would have gotten ice cream. And I would have taken a moment to acknowledge the sadness. To talk about my feelings, and theirs. They didn't need to know all my grief and depression, but it would have been nice to acknowledge that I had emotions. That I hurt too. Instead, I put on my strong, all-is-well mask and pushed onward.

This made it harder for us to get as close as we could have. With honesty and vulnerability, our relationship would have been better. The familiar tsunami of guilt washed over me. I wished I could have been the dad they deserved.

It's not too late.

Maybe it wasn't, but that meant change.

We reached the mountaintop ridge with views for miles. A sea of dark green Douglas fir and western hemlock blanketed the earth, rolling from one peak to the next. Gray, granite peaks of the North Cascades pierced the canopy, standing above the trees, some dusted with snow. Ancient batholith formations, created when oceanic plates slid under the continental plate millions of years ago, stretched forever into the distance.

This was the spot where, on that fateful day, I had intended to turn around. I felt an ecstatic pang in my chest. Here I was, at the top! I made it! And I was continuing onward. For the first time, a glimmer of hope, a small belief that I could finish, sparked inside.

I was forced to celebrate this moment alone in my head. I hadn't shared with Chris what had happened that weekend, keeping it secret from everyone. I needed to open up with him, to change the pattern, but this wasn't the moment. Or so I let myself believe in order to avoid the conversation.

Long, easy downhills lay ahead. The worst this section had to offer was behind me. I felt a need to move, to push forward, to feed on the hope and let it fuel me as far as possible. As I picked up the pace, Chris matched, pushing our bodies in silence.

I had been so afraid to let my crew down or disappoint Chris and Jenni that I had hidden my truth from them. I spent most of my life trying to outrun my fears, but I was coming to see I would never get ahead because I was carrying them with me. They would always be right there, no matter how far or fast I ran, until I let them go.

That was an interesting thought. What if I set down everything I was carrying? All the responsibility for others. The weight they hadn't even asked me to hold. All the worries about if I was strong enough. Fear I was a burden on the people around me. I was running from so much. Maybe, just maybe, I didn't have to.

My life to this point had been spent finding happiness where I was, accepting what I had. The problem was, now that I was giving myself a chance to think about what I actually wanted, where I wanted to be, I was coming up blank. I knew enduring well, it had been my whole life. What if I used my strength, experience, and knowledge to endure and go after what I wanted instead?

An image of an eagle came into my mind, and I imagined the freedom of flying. Of floating on the wind, flowing with the currents. Moving easily toward the horizon, where I sensed there was comfort waiting for me. Looking from this mountain ridge out over the tops of seemingly endless green pines, I envisioned looking over the world with a peace I'd never known as I traveled toward what felt good. Suddenly, though, things shifted as I contemplated what I might be leaving behind, and the vision came crashing down to the ground.

This was real for me. If I found my own dream and chased after it, if I spoke up for my truth and needs, then I risked ending relationships in my life, including Jenni. That meant being alone, unwanted. No one to validate my existence and accept me. No validation of the worth this lonely kid had been craving his entire life. I may feel judged and criticized in my relationship, but at least I wasn't alone.

"We're almost there," Chris said with excitement.

At first, I was confused how he knew, but then I heard it too. The sounds of people and movement. I could smell burritos, or at least all the wonderful things that would go inside the one that would soon be in my stomach. The aid station was just ahead.

I made it!

I'd conquered the Lewis River section!

One hundred thirty-one miles down, just sixty-nine to go. I giggled to myself at the distance. My mind was getting giddy and slow, but still functioning.

"Whoop!" I yelled in exhilaration, making Chris laugh as we burst through the trees.

Council Bluff aid station. 4:22 PM Sunday. The time wasted in the last aid station, the long uphill, and my tired body were slowing me down. I was now pushing the far edges of my estimated times, but not critically. I might take longer to finish, but it wouldn't stop me. Still, I made a mental note to watch the clock.

Jenni waited with the wagon and a surprise sign featuring Dwayne "The Rock" Johnson with the words "No, YOU rock!" We'd loaded the car together, but somehow, she managed to sneak it in there, bringing it out at the perfect time. I felt a wave of gratitude as I gave her a kiss, then looked her right in the eyes and said, "Thank you."

She smiled big, responding with our now repetitive dialogue. "Food?"

"Yes! Burrito?"

Out on the trail, I hadn't felt hungry, but now that I could smell the wonderful food, it hit hard and fast. While she was getting me something to eat, Chris and I sat down, an extraordinary pleasure, rivaled only by the giant burrito I wolfed down just a few minutes later.

"You want another one?" Jenni asked.

"Can I?" I asked, tentatively.

"Yes, they'll give you as many as you want!"

"Then hell yeah!" I said happily.

I was still hungry, it was as if the first burrito hadn't even happened. This made sense. I'd only eaten a handful of trail mix, a few protein bars, some sugary electrolytes, and a burrito in the last sixty hours, all while running almost non-stop. What didn't make sense was that I needed to poo again. Having eaten so little food, I couldn't imagine what was trying to get out, but it was happening.

"Where's the bathroom?" I asked a volunteer.

I hoped for another campground bathroom but would happily settle for a porta-potty.

"There's a shovel over there. Hike that way and find a spot off the trail. Dig down at least six inches and cover it well, please!" she said with a smile.

I paused. How bad did I really need to go? I had never had to squat outside to go before. There had always been some sort of facility I could use, however crude. I was exhausted and scared of accidentally making a mess on myself. Plus, every step down that trail meant extra steps, and I wasn't looking to take one more than I had to at this point.

My bowels shifted, letting me know they weren't kidding. I picked up the shovel, complete with a roll of toilet paper around the end, and walked as short a distance as I felt was appropriate. It was hard to dig, but I managed to get eight or so inches deep. I pulled my shorts down around my ankles, holding them forward with one hand to keep them out of the way, and squatted over the hole as best I could. I felt silly, and my muscles were complaining loudly as the stretching felt painful.

OK, bombs away!

I mentally crossed my fingers, then relaxed my muscles. Shockingly to me, everything slid right out, fast and easy. I felt instant relief, knowing the deed was done. I wiped, mustered my willpower to stand up, followed by a quick body check. No mess anywhere, I was spotless.

This is how people are supposed to do it!

Relieved, I filled the hole with dirt and headed back to the aid station to wash my hands.

Chris and Jenni were waiting there with my second burrito. It eased the hunger slightly while I contemplated the path ahead.

Jenni would pace this leg, which I looked forward to because she had been such a positive force during this race. It would be nice to share this part of the adventure together. This was a shorter section, only 9.8 miles.

Only, haha.

Two miles gentle up, one and a half miles down, really big uphill, then mild rollers for a total of 2,113 feet going up and 1,781 down.

I jolted awake, or back to consciousness, unsure how much time had passed or how long I'd been sitting. Too long, clearly. Chris and Jenni weren't in much better shape, time to get going. I needed to move for all our sakes.

I forced myself up and out of the chair, bringing the two of them out of their stupors. After double-checking that Chris could reach the next aid station, Jenni and I started by walking, needing a little time for my muscles to loosen and my body to warm up a bit. It would be dark before we finished.

"Hey, I really appreciate everything you've been doing to help, thank you," I said, making eye contact.

She smiled. "You're welcome."

"It's kinda crazy, isn't it? That we're out here, doing this?"

"I know! It's been hard, but also amazing. And fun," she responded.

"Everything going all right on your end? I haven't had much of a chance to ask."

"Yup, everything's going as planned. Jeff should be here to pace you the next section, and Keith and your mom are on track to be here after that. Been a couple of hiccups, but overall things are good!"

We ran for a few minutes in silence. Things felt good, like we were finally on the same page again.

"You're doing great!" she suddenly said. "I can't believe how awesome you are."

This was the drug I craved. Her approval, acknowledgment of this major feat, her pride in me.

Is she proud of you, or is she happy this will make us both look good to others?

I felt instant guilt at the thought, not wanting to taint the moment. But there was a reason it crossed my mind. It was the battle we had been silently fighting. She wanted to look good and needed to keep me in line to do it. I wanted appreciation and approval. Neither of us discussed feelings, wants, needs, or why. This race had brought a break in hostilities, but not a complete ceasefire.

Since I'd first asked her to pace me, I worried that my depleted condition at this stage of the race might lead to saying the wrong thing. Or, even worse, the honest thing. Would I speak my fears and frustrations aloud if too tired? I spent so much time being who others wanted that I wasn't sure who I really was. What if the real me emerged? What if I was mean? Or not a good person?

As we started running, I noted I was exhausted, and all my defenses were down. Yet the "real" me was the person who'd been listening to her advice, laughing with Chris. Dave, the aid station worker, had befriended the real me. The smiles, gratitude, and happiness were all who I was deep inside. I liked this version and so did others. I wanted more of this person.

We reached the top of the climb and turned onto a wide fire road passing through thinning trees, revealing a spectacular night sky. Stars filled the heavens, more than I'd seen in years. Being far from civilization meant little light pollution. We slowed to a walk in silent wonder for the next mile downhill, soaking it all in. It was a magical moment I'd never forget, no matter how fried my brain was. Eventually, the dragon markers led us back into the forest, obscuring the heavens.

In the silence, I noticed my shoes squished.

Why are my feet still wet?

This many miles since the river crossings, they shouldn't be more than damp. I didn't have an answer, and it didn't matter in this moment, so I let my thoughts drift back to the discovery that with all defenses down, I was a good, happy person.

I remembered my mother once saying that I was the eternal optimist. "If you were on the *Titanic*," she'd said, "you'd be saying 'we got this!' while organizing and helping people."

She wasn't wrong. This was the optimist in me, but also the person who needed to appear in control when things went wrong. The "everything's okay" face, worrying about others to avoid burdening them with caring for me. The mask my mother taught me to wear.

Then came the day it slipped. Mom asked how I was doing on the phone. My instinct was to say all was well and move on. This time, I paused.

"Not good."

Everything poured out. The divorce, work struggles, decreasing income, pushing away friends, loneliness, and depression.

"Thank you for finally telling me! I've known for a long time that things were rough. I wished you would talk to me about it, but didn't want to pressure you."

I believed I'd hidden my struggles well, but it was more transparent than I imagined. We had a good long talk, and I agreed not to hold back again. After this, we were closer.

I knew I should take this into other relationships. Especially with my kids, to break the cycle. A passage I'd read in college from psychologist Terry Real echoed in my mind as we ran through the dark in silence. "Family pathology rolls from generation to generation like a fire in the woods, taking down everything in its path until one person, in one generation, has the courage to turn and face the flames." I would have to march into the fire, hoping it was not too late to save my children from the burn.

I needed to open up with Jenni too. We could both let go of the walls keeping us from truly going all in. Yet, admitting this to her meant I would have to do my part, and I wasn't sure I was ready.

Entering the last few miles of rolling hills, I looked at Jenni and felt a radiating glow of appreciation. This was the Jenni I fell in love with. Fun, adventurous, loving, and caring for me. I wanted her to feel the same love from me.

"Make sure you are getting sleep and taking care of yourself in between aid stations," I said, knowing from long experience that it was easy to neglect the self when caring for others.

"I can't," she answered simply.

"Yes, you can!" I urged.

"No, I can't," she said, exasperated. "There's not enough time. When you leave, I have to get everything back to the car and load it up. Then drive out to where there's phone service and check that your pacers will be here. I have to figure out how to get to the next place you're going because many aid stations are only found using GPS coordinates on unpaved roads. When I finally get there, I have to unload everything and be ready when you come in. I try to sleep when you do, but I can't completely relax in case you wake up and need something."

I was stunned. For me, there were several hours between aid stations, sometimes eight or more. In that time, I traveled fifteen to twenty miles. Driving from one aid station to the next, however, could be daunting. Often it was on the other side of a mountain or another obstacle that had to be navigated around, slowly on back roads. It could take a few hours just to drive from one stop to the next. It was not unheard of for crews to drive well over 500 miles to support their runner traveling only 200.

I'd assumed she had plenty of time to relax and rest as I was slowly making my way on the trail. Now I saw she was working as hard as I was, just getting from one aid station to the next. This didn't include everything she was doing to manage the countless details. To prevent even the smallest thing from derailing my entire event.

Headlamp batteries, for instance. One might suffice, but could malfunction, so I carried backup. Runners without crew would use drop bags, yet that required six to eight expensive batteries that were hopefully still functional when needed. She was changing mine out at every station, then recharging them, ensuring I was ready.

That was just headlamps. So many details needed attention for this to work. Jenni was executing perfectly, taking such good care that I didn't see it. I'd wanted for nothing so far. It was hard for me to accept being taken care of, to be worried about. It went against all I knew.

"Thank you. So much. I greatly appreciate all you're doing, and I know it's a lot. Do as best you can to take care of yourself. I want you to be safe." It felt not enough, yet it was full of sincerity.

"You're welcome."

I saw her smile, appreciating the recognition. Ahead glowed the lights of the next aid station. We picked up the pace, blissfully unaware things were about to fall apart.

10

I was excited to be coming into the Chain of Lakes aid station, ready to take another break. I'd completed over 140 miles at this point and knew I had more in me. The dark night silhouetted the trees, black against the starlit sky. Jenni and I made our way along a dirt road lined with cars belonging to volunteers and crews, headlamps cutting through the cedar-scented air.

Noticing movement in a car beside me, I glanced over, forgetting I was wearing a headlamp and shining my light brightly into the vehicle. There, like a deer in the headlights, was my next pacer, Jeff. He looked petrified. Not the expression one hopes to see from their guide through the next seventeen miles of dark wilderness, but I attributed it to surprise and moved on.

Chris escorted me to a chair while Jenni topped off my water and prepared my pack. The sandwich they offered here was adequate, though I found myself mourning the absence of burritos with the sort of intensity usually reserved for the bottom of a bag of chips.

"You might need to check on Jeff," Chris noted.

"What's up?" I inquired.

"Something about the rivers. He seems kinda freaked out."

I had slept less than ninety minutes in the last seventy-two hours, and exhaustion was finally presenting its bill. My brain could only process the basics. Eat. Drink. Keep moving. Anything else required too much computing power for my overtaxed CPU.

It took me several seconds of staring and blinking before my mind cleared enough to make sense of the gibberish on my watch. It was 8:38 PM on Sunday night. This meant behind schedule by a couple of hours, though I hadn't the faintest idea where the time had gone.

I paused for a volunteer to check my feet. As she pulled my shoes and socks off, I noted they were still wet, though they should have been mostly dry by now. As she looked my feet over, Jeff approached with the expression of a man about to confess to a crime.

"I can't do it," Jeff said, fear flickering in his eyes. "It's the rivers. The water. I can't go across."

"Can I ask why?"

"I was kayaking a few months ago, and it tipped over. I fell in the water, couldn't get back in the boat, and I kept sinking. I thought I could do this, but I can't."

This leg had four significant water crossings without bridges. Depending on the weather, the water could be as high as waist-deep. To prepare each pacer, I provided all the details I had for their section. I gave them the mileage, the elevation gain and loss, and descriptions about what we might encounter.

I could see the volunteer quietly listening as she worked on my feet. I reached down and put my hand over Jeff's to comfort him while looking him sincerely in the eyes. "It's okay, I've got this. Thank you for telling me, and please don't worry about it."

He was visibly relieved, having being absolved from his duty.

"Thank you," he said as he got up and disappeared into the night, headed back to his car.

His role to play, now forfeited, was over. He would return to his car and head home. I would have welcomed him to stay and help in other ways, but I knew his self-imposed shame would speed the abrupt retreat. I felt empathy, knowing the pain of disappointing another.

I caught the volunteer's sympathetic eyes. They echoed my sense that gently letting him off the hook had been the right thing to do, even though it meant I'd be traveling the next section alone. I had mentally prepared for this possibility because there's always a chance someone would get lost or delayed. I was grateful to have pacers, yet I knew I could not rely on them for my success.

Jenni and Chris materialized from the shadows, clearly upset.

"It's okay," I said immediately. "It's much better he backed out now than at the first river crossing. It's not ideal, but I'm glad he spoke up."

"He should have said something a long time ago," Jenni declared.

"Definitely! Now is not the time!" Chris concurred.

"Better now than halfway through," I repeated, though neither seemed ready to accept this practical wisdom.

I slipped my foot into the first shoe, feeling the new, dry sock instantly saturate.

That isn't right.

I had much bigger things to worry about than wet shoes with what little brain power I had left. I dismissed any concern as the second shoe did the same.

The section ahead would be more difficult without Jeff, but I wouldn't have to carry him through it, a relief.

Jeff had been honest and very vulnerable when he honored his need to step away. He'd gotten on a plane, rented a car, driven hours to meet me, then made the very difficult decision to do the right thing for himself. It is not the choice I would have made. I would've pushed through, attempting to be strong enough. That's what my crew clearly expected of him. I was running 200 miles, he was going home.

Was it possible Jeff is stronger than me?

It was now habit for me to walk through any hurricane that came my way, attempting to not even blink. Perhaps seeking shelter was the smarter, stronger choice, even if it meant judgment from others.

Is it possible to give myself that same grace?

Something to think about, but right now I needed to move. Without Jeff, I would be doing a third night alone in the woods. The section ahead included 17.3 miles with four major river crossings, starting with a mile and a half descent to the first crossing, then nine miles of rolling hills carved by glaciers, before five miles of steep incline. There would be an out-and-back to Elk Peak, a volcanic remnant from the Cascades' tumultuous geological past, ending with an easy descent into the next aid station. There would be 3,806 feet of elevation gain total and 3,780 loss.

The brief time sitting down and the food had helped. Perhaps I was rallying in response to Jeff's departure. Whatever the reason, I went on autopilot, letting gravity do the work as I descended through switchbacks designed to keep the grade manageable on the steep slopes. My mind was pleasantly free of thoughts, which was nice after all the thinking it had been doing the past few days.

Suddenly, the trail ended. Trees and bushes blocked my way. My brain, like a calculator with dying batteries, struggled to make sense of this development. I turned to the right. There was the trail, leading up.

Up?

My brain paused.

I guess it makes sense. I've been going down for a while.

An alarm rang in the back of my consciousness, but my muddled mind couldn't decode the warning.

After several switchbacks, the trail evened out, and the alarms became louder.

Am I going the right way?

The question met silence. I turned around and started back down, then doubted that decision. If I was wrong, I'd have to climb back up, wasted energy I couldn't spare. I turned around and started moving back up the trail. Within a few minutes, I started to doubt myself again. I stood for a moment motionless, looking back and forth like a broken compass.

The course, it's on the app in my phone.

Yes, that was it. I pulled out my phone and saw an arrow, indicating me, on the map, there on the trail. But I didn't know if the arrow pointed the direction I was traveling, or the way I should go. I zoomed in and out, but I couldn't see the aid stations or anything else to indicate which was the right way. I tried moving one direction then the other, but nothing changed, so it didn't help.

I put the phone away and started back down the trail for almost half a mile before changing my mind and going back up it again. I was about to turn around yet again when I realized I wasn't confident enough to make a choice. Going back and forth wasn't helping, so I stood there, paralyzed by indecision.

The cold started seeping in, causing me to shiver. I had to make a choice. I started uphill, that was the first decision I'd made, and I should stick to it. After a while, I saw a headlamp coming toward me.

Rescued!

Dark hair tucked under a hat, hydration pack, sweat-stained clothes, and dirt-covered legs, the universal uniform of the long-distance sufferer. Seeing me traveling toward her left a look of confusion on her face.

"Are you headed to Klickitat?" I asked, referring to the aid station ahead.

"No, Chain of Lakes," she replied.

"That's where I just came from. You're going there? We're supposed to be headed to Klickitat."

"That's where I came from," she said with conviction.

It did not make any sense. She should be going toward Klickitat from here. Two exhausted and sleep-deprived people were not the right ones to be figuring this out, it was the proverbial blind leading the blind, but there was no one else.

"You came from Klickitat? And you're going to Chain of Lakes? You're sure?" I asked.

"Yes." There was no doubt in her voice.

I knew for certain we should be traveling toward Klickitat. If she was positive she had left there, then we needed to go back that way.

"Then you're going the wrong way. We should be going this way." I pointed up the trail, the direction I had been going.

I passed her and started up the trail. She continued to stand there, unsure, as I moved away. I briefly thought about insisting she follow me, but I wasn't going to force her into any mistake I may be making. If I ended up in the right place, I'd let the aid station people know so they could send someone to find her. If I came to the wrong place, I wouldn't mislead her.

I had slowed down to a walk long ago, the burst of energy I'd started with totally gone. Doubt continued to swirl in my mind. After about a mile, I came to an aid station. I recognized it right away. Chain of Lakes, the place I had left from. There were two volunteers standing a short distance away, looking at me curiously.

To be certain, I called out, "Is this Chain of Lakes?"

"Yes!" they shouted back in unison.

"Thank you!" I responded, then turned around and headed back down the trail.

Now that I had the right direction, I started running again, but all the urgency I'd started with was gone. I had no idea how much time I'd wasted wandering in circles, but my finishing time was now thoroughly screwed. How much time and energy had I wasted, and would it leave me with enough to finish?

Remarkably, I never thought about quitting, nor did I get upset. I had come into the race knowing things would not go to plan. This was where the fifth step I had created came into play: to adapt. I had to let go of "the plan" and flow with what was. Had I not anticipated this, it could have been devastating. I might have become paralyzed in my exhausted mind, unable to adjust to the reality. I could easily have used this as an excuse to walk away. Instead, I was prepared, ready to change with whatever the race would throw my way.

I could have been mad at Jeff, who would have kept me on course. This could have broken me, but I did my usual pushing through, which had paid dividends this round. This neurosis of mine was a good thing under the right circumstances. I didn't need to completely get rid of this part of me, it was integral to who I was and my success. And it was important to learn when to push and when to let go.

I caught up with the woman I'd confused earlier, walking slowly toward me with the defeated air of someone contemplating surrender.

"This way," I said, pointing the correct direction this time.

I could see the doubt in her eyes. I'd already told her to go one way, now I was telling her the opposite.

"I ended up in the wrong place, this is the right way," I said.

I could sense her contemplating whether to continue or return to the aid station and quit. I wasn't going to let that happen on my account.

"Let's go!" I said authoritatively, with more enthusiasm than I felt, and ran past her.

She turned and followed. We descended through the switchbacks in silence, me contemplating my earlier mistake, trying to figure out what had happened. Then I saw it. I'd hugged the right side of a wide turn, mistaking the continuation of the trail as a left turn onto a separate path. Had I turned left instead of right, I wouldn't have made the error. Narrowed vision, exhausted brain, and a fateful random choice led me astray. Simple as that, but costly. I ran at least two extra miles, probably more, and lost a lot of time.

You'll be first place for the 208.5 mile race!

I laughed quietly to myself, humor my most effective coping mechanism.

It did not take long before we reached the first river crossing. We had not said a word to each other since resuming the run, yet I felt a connection. Two people on a mission. I stepped into the ice-cold water, which helped wake me out of my stupor, the current strong against our weakened legs.

This first river crossing ended up being about mid-thigh for me, a little deeper for her. The bottom was smooth basalt, polished by centuries of glacial runoff from the surrounding peaks. I heard her slip but not fall. I looked back, and wordlessly we reached out to hold hands before continuing across, then let go and continued quietly. I led and she stayed ten feet behind, never challenging my pace.

The trail started uphill, as it always seemed to do after a water crossing, and I slowed down, water squishing from my shoes. I glanced back to see if she wanted to pass and go faster, but she was right there, matching my pace. She looked up with "all's good" implied on her face, so I just kept going.

The sky lightened as we crossed the second river, much shallower, only coming up to my calves. I glanced back to ensure she was safely across before we continued without a word. We moved in silence through the next two big water crossings, the sun breaking over the mountains as we crossed the last one. My shoes squished, water squeezing out with each step.

That's unusual.

They should be wet, but not squishy and oozing water this far from the river crossing. Of course, I didn't give it another thought.

I needed to slow down, yet with her behind me, I was feeling pressured, triggering feelings of being chased. It made me anxious that whatever pace I went, she remained consistently ten feet behind.

I should have used words, explained what I was feeling, asking her what she wanted. But that would have meant admitting I couldn't carry her, contradicting the whole point of being out here to prove I could do hard things. It would have meant asking for what I needed, something I'd never mastered. Since I couldn't speak up, I sought another solution. A moment of inspiration hit.

"I need to pee," I announced, heading into a small clearing.

She hesitated, uncertain whether to wait or continue. I could see she was stumped. It would be weird to stop and stand there while I peed, but she was hesitating to go on alone.

"You go ahead, I'll be right behind you," I encouraged.

She carried on without a word. I paused, waiting for enough time to pass, then got on the trail at a pace my body could maintain. Normal etiquette is when one runner stopped, the other would go ahead, then slow down or walk until the person behind caught up. I didn't mind following, I just didn't want the pressure of leading.

Either she was faster than me or decided not to wait, but after several minutes, there was still no sign of her. I felt bad, but I had to take care of my own needs. In the past, I would have run until I blew up. This time, I did better for myself, though it was still handled poorly. We never said more than a few words to each other, and I did not get her name, yet I missed her company as I continued alone.

I plodded through the mountains, my mind too far gone for coherent thought, winding through stands of western red cedar and Pacific silver fir, their understory thick with salmonberry and Oregon grape. I passed through an empty campground, oddly deserted for a Sunday morning in August. Admittedly, there were parts inside that wanted people to be here witnessing me accomplishing this feat. Since childhood, I'd craved recognition, validation from other people taking notice.

Another large piece of baggage I'd brought into the relationship with Jenni. I relied on her to see me and provide validation. The challenge was that, over this past year, I felt like she was giving me less as I became increasingly more desperate for it.

Just like with the woman I'd been running with, I failed to talk about what I was feeling and needed. Instead, I tried to lead by example. When she was pummeled by insecurity, I persisted in sharing the true vision of her that I saw. She was an amazing person and worthy.

The fantasy was that she would feel better, see everything I had done for her, and return the validation. But it was just that, a fantasy. Like me, she would never feel good enough. I would always have to be filling that tank, a Sisyphean task. On top of that, she was not getting the message that I craved what I was giving. Without a better plan, I carried on.

I was startled by a large, dark object lying next to the trail ahead. As I got closer, I could see it was a person. I was worried the woman I'd been lost with had gotten hurt. But no, it was a man, hoodie pulled up over his face. When he moved slightly, I knew he was okay, so I ran past.

Some 200-mile runners nap alongside the trail. It wasn't something I felt comfortable doing. Knowing my luck, I'd inevitably choose an anthill or spiders' nest as a pillow. A few feet from him was an arrow made of sticks, a trick many trail nappers used. When he awoke disoriented, the arrow would show him which way to go.

As I left him behind, I ruminated again on Jenni. By now, I was recycling my previous thoughts. Just like the symbol I'd learned in school with three chasing arrows in a triangle, I was going through the process but not creating anything new. I kept ending up with the same bottle I started with, regardless of what happened between.

I'd drift back to my forcibly independent childhood, realize I sucked at articulating my needs, and play this out in how I overcompensated by trying to fulfill others' needs, all the while avoiding big questions. As this version completed and began buffering for the replay, I looked up.

Bigfoot!

There he was, just off the left side of the trail ahead. Tall, reddish-brown, and furry, standing motionless. I knew it couldn't be real, but no matter how many times I blinked, the vision didn't change.

I must finally be hallucinating.

Most runners did at some point during the race, this was likely my moment.

As I got closer, he got a little less furry. His shape morphed, looking less creature-like. Then my eyes finally focused. It was merely a tall stump, very close in shape and color to Bigfoot, as the texture of the rotting red cedar gave it a hairy appearance. I felt justified in what I'd seen, though slightly disappointed it wasn't a proper hallucination. Not that I wanted to have one, but if I did, Bigfoot would have been a really cool one to have.

A small breeze drifted by and gave me a whiff of myself.

Ew!

I stunk. Really bad. Three days of sweat, dirt, and whatever else was adhering to me was making itself known. I picked the pace up slightly, trying to outrun my own stench.

The trees thinned as I climbed higher into the sub-alpine zone, where mountain hemlock and Pacific silver fir gave way to sparse groves of whitebark pine before surrendering to scrubby brush. Ahead was a sign with dragons attached, indicating the two-mile out-and-back to Elk Peak.

As I neared the top, the trail gave way to loose shale. Volcanic debris from ancient eruptions that slid treacherously underfoot. I had to almost crawl the last thirty feet, which oddly felt good as it required different muscles. At the top, I stood alone, surrounded by tree-covered mountains as far as I could see.

Before the Bigfoot 200 appeared on my radar, I completed the San Francisco Triathlon at Alcatraz, which started from a large ferry boat bobbing next to the infamous island in the middle of the Bay. We could nearly reach out and touch the island on one side, while the city of San Francisco dominated the skyline on the other side. I jumped off the ferry into the cold water and started swimming for the city with the 800 other participants.

During the pre-race meeting, the race director passed on some wisdom for the difficult and legendary swim, warning us about unpredictable currents and providing landmarks in the city to swim toward.

"When you are about halfway across," the race director said, "stop for a few seconds to look around. You will be experiencing the Bay as only a handful of people ever will, seeing it from a perspective you will never get from a boat. Don't make the mistake of completing the swim and remembering nothing but the water in front of you."

I took his advice and stopped halfway to absorb the view, thinking how lucky I was to be there. Ever since, hard moments prompted me to slow down and take it all in. I didn't want to be so head-down occupied with my goal that I failed to experience the awe-inspiring journey. I paused there at Elk Peak, looking around, soaking up the sun, and taking a deep breath.

Mount Saint Helens dominated the southern horizon, where this adventure began a few days ago. To the southeast loomed Mount Hood with its pointed, snowcapped peak. Further east stood Mount Adams, round and white. After rounding Helen, the course had veered toward Adams before turning north, where Mount Rainier rose impressively. Somewhere between me and Rainier awaited the finish line. Serene moments like these renewed my love for running.

I stepped off to the side and peed. It was quite intentional. I wanted the mountain to know that in this moment, I had won. Despite being lost, alone, and exhausted, I'd made it here. Whatever else happened, this victory couldn't be taken away.

Sliding down the loose shale on my return, I had a pang of regret. Had I acted too triumphantly and angered the Trail Gods? Then I felt calm, as if they were telling me they understood. It wasn't done with malice or cockiness, but with humility and appreciation for meeting the challenge.

When I returned to the main trail, it was just over a mile of easy downhill to the next aid station. Feeling redeemed by the mountaintop victory, I settled into a quick, steady pace. Moving through the fresh morning air brought a moment of lightness and hope. A song popped into my head, which made me think of my son.

Chris had once played me this song called "The Grand Optimist" by City and Colour, which reminded him of me. It spoke of the artist's father, who would experience "burdensome times" yet always escape unscarred. I'd felt proud. I was an unrepentant optimist, but even more so, this reinforced the image of strength I'd tried so hard to present to the world.

Am I really unscarred?

In this moment, the song hit differently. Optimism was part of my strength, it had seen me through many rough times. Yet, unlike the father in the song, I was not unscathed. I just hid my scars well. Or liked to believe I did.

Chris knew I was carrying wounds, as did Joy, Jenni, my mother, and all my siblings. The only person I was fooling was myself, and I wasn't doing a great job of that. It was time to stop trying to be the strong person no one needed to worry about.

This didn't mean I wasn't strong, capable, and good. It meant that I also hurt sometimes. That I needed things too and wanted to be loved. It was okay to ask for reminders and reassurance when I needed them.

Finally hearing noises ahead, I knew the Klickitat aid station was close. After this ordeal, I needed sleep and food. One of the toughest sections of the race was next, and I planned to use this station for a much-needed reset.

Coming off the trail and onto the fire road, I saw two volunteers heading to the trailhead loaded with medical gear. They looked at my bib number, seeming confused. They stepped back and watched me go by before turning to follow me. Ahead were Jenni, Chris, and Keith, joining to pace the next section, with my mom, who had caught a ride with him. They all looked enormously relieved.

"What's going on?" I asked, aware of the tension in the air.

"They were just going to look for you," Jenni said, waving toward the volunteers.

"Why?"

"Everyone thought something happened. The last aid station said they saw you come back, then leave again. Your GPS tracker went offline, and you were supposed to be here several hours ago."

I hadn't stopped to think they would radio ahead to warn the people here, but I should have. It made sense. There was a whole team of volunteers whose job was to keep us safe, coming to find those who wandered off course or appeared to be in distress. This late in the race, even with a clearly marked trail, runners would run into the same difficulties I had. Some participants might be hallucinating at this point, in which case all bets were off for them staying on course. Had I thought of this, I would have explained before turning around and disappearing at the previous aid station.

I glanced at my watch, now Monday morning, several hours behind schedule. I had no clue what happened out there, time had dissipated.

"I got lost and turned around for a while, but I figured it out. Sorry, I didn't think anyone would be worried."

"We're just glad you're okay. What do you need?" Jenni asked.

"Sleep! Where's the tents?"

"Umm. There aren't any here." She seemed surprised I didn't know this. "Just the basics. Sleep station is the next one."

I looked at the table with water and snacks. This was a bare-minimum setup in a remote spot. No sleep. No burritos.

I was exhausted. Nearly twenty miles to the next aid station over very difficult terrain. Rest and a meal had been my motivation to get here, now the line had been moved. My tired brain was struggling as I stared off into the trees, wondering what to do. The ancient forest offered no answers.

Trail Gods, where are you now?

11

Klickitat aid station was set up on the side of a remote forest service fire road without a name, identified only by number on the special Forest Service maps I'd had to buy for Jenni in advance. It was challenging getting here, so the aid station was minimal. I was deflated and discouraged because the thought of food and sleep was the only thing that got me this far. Now there wasn't even a chair to sit on.

My cheap watch revealed it was 9:31 AM Monday morning, over eight hours past my worst-case estimate to arrive here. Seeing my distress, my crew went to action mode. Jenni ran to the Jeep to grab a folding camp chair I could painfully fold myself into, and Chris ran to get me a sandwich. Keith was working with the tracking volunteers, trying to figure out what happened to my GPS signal. My mom filled my water bottle.

This was mile 158, and fatigue had settled in long ago. My mind was completely shut down, leaving me lifeless and defeated.

"35!" boomed across the void of my mind.

"Dave!"

His shout shook my thoughts loose. I hadn't expected to see him.

"How you doing, man?"

"I'm tired. My feet are killing me," I croaked.

"Want me to take a look?"

"That'd be great, if you don't mind," I responded gratefully.

As Dave fetched supplies, I tried to take my shoes off. After a couple of fumbling tries, I finally got one off. Water squished and ran out as my foot was freed. This finally registered as worthy of investigation. I paid close attention as the second foot released the water, then studied the shoe, seeking a cause.

The revelation arrived with the dull impact of delayed comprehension. Back at Lewis River, I'd switched to a pair of waterproof trail shoes, thinking this would be good for the upcoming sections with lots of river crossings. What I hadn't considered was that these shoes were designed to keep out water from a shallow puddle, dew from the morning grass, light rain, or the occasional splash. They kept small amounts of water on the surface from getting inside, they were not meant to be submerged.

In the same way they kept water out, once the defenses were breached, these shoes held it all in. Like a medieval castle's moat system working in reverse, they'd trapped every drop for the last fifty miles. This is exactly why the "nothing new on race day" rule existed.

As I pulled off my soaked socks, Jenni gasped audibly. My feet were swollen, wrinkled, and so pale they were almost translucent. They looked like they belonged on a drowned body.

"Dude, your feet look like you're dead!" Dave exclaimed as he approached.

"I know," I replied.

"No, seriously, dude, they look like a corpse."

"Yup." There wasn't much to say about his medical assessment.

Dave went to work with tape as if he were preparing a mummy for eternal rest, covering all my feet instead of just the trouble spots. Jenni went to get a new pair of socks and the shoes I'd started in.

I'd eaten the sandwich and was still hungry, my body beginning to shiver as it cooled. Jenni quickly located blankets that I wrapped myself in like a particularly pitiful rescued dog.

Looking for something to lift my spirits, I tapped into my ever-ready sense of humor. I looked at Dave and feebly said, "I must be first, I can't see anyone ahead of me."

"Definitely!" he said, laughing at my joke as he stood up. Then he looked me in the eye with conviction and said, "I will see you at the finish."

I nodded, less certain than he was, as he turned and walked away.

Putting my shoes on felt like too much. The morning sun crested the trees, shining directly in my eyes. I pulled the blanket over my head and was instantly asleep, my corpse-feet protruding from the makeshift shroud. To a passing observer, I would appear recently deceased.

The sleep wasn't restful, more like a brief system shutdown. Eventually, I stirred with the reality that I was hemorrhaging time. I'd already burned hours being lost, and now I'd spent at least two more here. The clock ticked with persistence. I sat under the blanket, unmoving, as silence enveloped the area. Not even a bird call.

The arrival of another runner woke up the station, resuming activity and noise. Inspired, I threw off the blanket and struggled to sit up. I tugged my socks on over the tape, then managed to stuff my swollen feet into the shoes and get them tied. Keith helped me stand, my joints seizing like rusty hinges.

Some runners took ibuprofen, but I never had, partly because I heard it was hard on the liver during activity. The true reason for avoiding them, however, was since I ran for the pain, medications felt like cheating. If medication made it easier, was I really strong enough to do it? Without the aid of a pill, movement would help, so I forced myself to take a few unsteady steps as my crew packed up.

This would be a brutal section, one I had dreaded when preparing. 19.4 miles, hitting the race's highest elevation while covering 4,619 feet uphill and 4,685 feet down. I was in rough shape, but if I could make it through this section, everything after would be rolling hills and gentle descents to the finish.

The lost time meant another night on the trails. At least this time I wouldn't be alone, Keith was pacing me through terrain that demanded not only endurance but the relentless positivity he brought to even the darkest moments.

In addition to enjoying each other's company, we were each other's person to call when we wanted to do stupid things, like this race. I'd paced him through the last fifteen or so miles of his hundred-mile adventure. Most often, though, it was an invitation to join an event. Conversations would often begin with "Hey, there's this really brutal fifty-mile race in April, you in?"

We rarely said no, and when we did, it was most often due to scheduling issues. As a result, he and I had done many long races and crazy events together. I had intentionally asked him to pace me for this section, where I would need not only his endurance but also the fun he brought. He always had a smile and joke ready to go, one of the few people I knew who was as positive as I was, even in the worst of times. With all excuses gone, we started toward the trailhead.

"You got this, 35! See you at the finish!" I heard Dave yelling.

I threw a thumbs-up because words were too much at the moment. We moved into the thickening forest, fir and hemlock trunks rising straight and branchless before exploding into crowns that filtered morning light into a kaleidoscope. The volcanic soil, deposited by the Cascade mountain range's periodic tantrums over millennia, provided excellent drainage and a soft path. It was silent and peaceful.

The trail immediately became a series of long, steep climbs followed by equally punishing descents. The sort of terrain that makes one question the sanity of those who originally forged these trails.

We settled into a comfortable silence in this sacred space, the trees forming a cathedral-like atmosphere. Our footfalls were barely audible on the soft dirt path, playing out a quiet beat that gradually produced a trance-like state.

From this running meditation, it dawned on me that despite my deep appreciation for Jenni's wonderful support, it was foolish to think that completing this race would somehow fix our relationship. That everything would magically be better, simply because I ran really far.

You're holding onto the potential of the relationship, not the current state.

I was ignoring the present, clinging to the past when things had been good, and living for a future I hoped would be better. But wishing wasn't going to make it happen. If I wanted a different future, I would have to start addressing all the hard things I'd been avoiding.

I stumbled on a tree root, the simple act of thinking and running now requiring more processing power than I could muster. I let all thoughts go. Exhaustion was overtaking me in waves. My brain was shutting down, leaving only the basic function of placing one foot in front of the other. The soft footfalls were like a metronome, sounding off each step with a slow, steady beat.

Suddenly, I jolted alert.

Was I just asleep?

There was no memory of the last several minutes, and nothing around me looked familiar. I shook it off, then it happened again a few short minutes later. I was sleep-running, moving forward on complete autopilot while taking micro naps.

As darkness fell, I started power walking, or perhaps aggressive trudging was more accurate. Time was warping around me like something from a physics experiment gone wrong. My watch displayed numbers that appeared like indecipherable hieroglyphics. I kept falling asleep as I was moving. Step after step, endlessly forward, with Keith behind me.

"Do you hear that?" I suddenly asked, awakened from my stupor.

"What?" Keith replied.

"There's voices. Up ahead, on the left. I think it's the aid station. Or a campground. I can hear them."

Keith tilted his head, straining to listen. "I don't hear anything."

"It's there," I said with confidence. "We must be getting close. I can hear them."

I picked up the pace, running even faster. Voices were pulling me forward like a siren song, promising food and sleep. We continued, but the voices were not getting any closer.

As the trees on our left thinned, revealing a dark void that suggested a significant drop, the voices began to fade. I peered wistfully off into the darkness, but couldn't see anything.

"I can't hear the voices anymore," I complained.

"I never heard them," Keith replied, concern creeping into his voice.

Between the two of us, he was significantly more likely to be right. I was probably hallucinating from sheer desire for the aid station to appear. We pressed on, the trail narrowing dangerously close to the edge, the soft earth on the left side with the drop crumbling beneath our feet. We leaned right and avoided putting weight on the left, creating an awkward, limping gait that made my hip ache.

The discomfort made the micro naps stop. With the hint of consciousness, I thought to ask about my mother.

"How is Mom doing? Is she okay?" I asked.

"Yeah, she seems to be fine. She slept a bit in the car, and she's smiling and happy," he replied.

I worried about her stamina for this endurance event, then remembered she'd raised eight kids and was tougher than anyone I knew.

Growing up, I'd never doubted her love. It was constant as gravity, though often just as invisible. She said it often, and it was evident in all her actions. She worked hard and sacrificed so that we could eat and have a roof over our heads. We all revered and adored her. No one ever said a bad word about Mom, nor mentioned anything that might be missing.

Only in the past few years was I able to admit that, between working multiple jobs, raising eight children, and her own struggles with depression, individual attention for any of us was scarce. Love existed like the sun behind clouds. Always there, but not always accessible when needed.

Just as I learned to take care of my own needs, I learned not to depend on receiving love. Like one couldn't solely depend upon solar panels for electricity, especially here in the Pacific Northwest. Knowing the love existed behind the cloud cover became enough. I would soak it up when it came, like the rays of the sun through a break in the clouds on a stormy day, knowing it wouldn't last long.

That's why you stay with Jenni.

The thought arrived unbidden but accurate. I knew Jenni loved me and believed that knowledge was enough. When I felt alone or undesirable, I blamed it on cloud covering rather than examining the relationship's fundamental weather patterns.

This dynamic worked both ways. It had to be difficult being with someone who operated independently of love, someone who never allowed a partner to feel truly needed. Breaking this cycle would mean learning to receive love, to trust it would be there when I needed it. I didn't know how to do that.

I could hear voices again. They were back. I almost said something, but I knew Keith was already worried about me, so I kept my mouth shut.

"I hear those voices!" Keith said excitedly.

"Good, I'm not completely crazy yet!"

Within minutes, we emerged from darkness into the lights of Twin Sisters aid station. Mile 177.5, with the toughest sections behind me. My watch read 11:37 PM Monday night.

Unless something went catastrophically wrong, I was going to finish.

The moment of elation vanished as I smelled bacon sizzling. I made a beeline for the food tent, forgetting about Jenni, Chris, my mom, and even Keith. As I ordered a burrito with everything, they approached. Jenni led me to a chair while Chris waited for my burrito.

The logistics that went into making this race happen were quite spectacular, especially at these full aid stations. They brought in canopies, numerous cooking stoves, and enough food to feed the small army comprised of volunteers, hungry runners, and crew. The volunteers worked diligently to ensure everyone was well fed, cooking food quickly and to order. They rivaled the best camp cooks under grueling conditions. Many of them slept as little as the runners, sacrificing to take care of us as we came in at all hours of the day and night.

Keith was grabbing both of us some hot soup to warm up. My mom sat next to me in supportive silence. I could not think about anything other than food and sleep as Jenni wrapped a blanket around me.

I mindlessly took a sip of the soup Keith handed me, then felt something wet on my left hand. I glanced down to see it shaking uncontrollably, spilling soup everywhere. I watched it happen with detachment, as if observing someone else's malfunctioning appendage.

I looked at Keith, watching me with a look of confusion. He quickly realized it wasn't intentional, grabbing the cup away from me. We all watched my hand shake for another ten seconds or so before it cautiously returned to normal.

Sleep deprivation can disrupt the body's natural hormonal balances, leading to muscle spasms. I knew that much from pre-race research. I didn't want to explore the possibilities beyond that simple explanation, especially not at this moment. No one else wanted to voice what had just happened either, or whether it warranted concern. Instead, we sat in stunned silence until Chris arrived with my food a few seconds later.

I reached out intentionally with my left hand to take the burrito Chris held, testing the equipment. Everything seemed operational now, so I started stuffing the burrito into my face as fast as I could. Before I was halfway done, I asked for a second, and when that was delivered, a third. I wasn't full, but finally I didn't feel hungry.

Without my Garmin watch, I had no idea how many calories I was burning through, but it had to be over 10,000 a day, likely much more. I hadn't eaten much at all the first couple days out here. Even with these three burritos in my belly, I had to be several thousand calories in the hole just today. Tens of thousands of calories short over the entire event. I should write a book, I thought to myself, called *The Bigfoot Diet: One Way to Lose Some Weight, Though Not Recommended.*

As we sat there, I was sure we were talking, but had no idea what anyone, including myself, was saying. Everything felt detached, as if I was overhearing conversation from another room.

With food in my belly, sleep was next on my agenda. I collapsed in a sleeping tent with instructions to wake me in ninety minutes, the maximum I felt I could afford with the clock still ticking toward cutoff times.

The thin pads and scratchy wool blankets felt luxurious, a testament to how dramatically perspective can shift when basic needs go unmet for extended periods. This was my last thought.

Ninety minutes later, Jenni shook me awake. I opened my eyes and saw her above me, but it felt like looking through someone else's eyes. As if watching a point-of-view movie shot. I observed this character getting up, stepping out of the tent, and looking at the early morning light starting to appear above the mountains to the east. He ambled to a chair. Along the bottom of the screen, I envisioned the subtitle: Day four.

Around the fire, several runners huddled like zombies, staring vacantly off into space with dead eyes. No one said a word. It felt like eons since the first aid station, everyone buzzing with energy in a party atmosphere.

I sat wrapped in blankets, watching things happen around me, unaware of time. Then I noticed Chris preparing to accompany me. I was supposed to do this sixteen-mile leg alone, but Jenni must have conspired to prevent another solo navigation disaster. A wave of gratitude washed over me.

Only twenty-nine miles left.

The thought was ridiculous, more than a marathon remained, yet after 177.5 miles, everything was relative. This next leg contained five miles of easy rolling hills, an out-and-back to the top of Pompey Peak, followed by ten miles of gentle downhill. I finally truly believed I would finish.

The excitement of going with Chris revived me. I got up, and we headed into the trees as the sun was coming up over the mountains.

My muscles were tight from overuse and abbreviated sleep, yet they didn't fail me as we plodded off into the trees. Before long, Chris and I entered into a beautiful pasture bathed in morning sunlight, and my spirits lifted. The sun reflected off a small alpine lake while tall green grass waved softly in the wind, birds providing nature's soundtrack to complete the scene. We stopped, awestruck, in reverent observation, soaking the moment in.

This meadow represented everything magnificent about trail running, moments of transcendent beauty that exist only in that one moment for the observer, unrepeatable and precious. My body loosened, aches and pains returning to background noise as we drifted through the meadow.

"I will never forget that," Chris said with awe.

"Me either. That was amazing," I echoed.

As we returned to forest cover, Chris asked how I was doing.

"Never better!" I responded, only the hint of a lie to it.

A strategy I'd adopted years ago. Positive answers kept my mindset strong and made others smile, returning the energy.

I don't remember where I heard it, but a phrase popped into my mind. "Today is the best day of my life," I said aloud. "And tomorrow will be better."

Chris laughed, and I felt a giant grin spread across my face. This moment with my son was worth every mile it took to get here.

The landscape shifted to widely spaced Ponderosa pine and Douglas fir with thick understory. The ground cover, consisting of kinnikinnick, beargrass, and huckleberry bushes, soon obscured the trail, making it difficult to follow. Much of this course was extremely remote. I suspected parts saw more traffic during race weekend than the rest of the year combined.

We followed the dragons as we bushwhacked through the underbrush with our legs, serving the role of machete, accumulating small scrapes and cuts. My body was too numb to register pain from these minor additions to my collection of wounds. I was moving at a good pace, but still hadn't found the energy to run. Jenni might worry if we took too long, but there was little I could do. Hopefully, the GPS was working, and they could track us if necessary.

Emerging from the brush, we came onto a long, flat trail that hugged the curve of the slope. I could see far into the distance as the path wound through an obstacle course of fallen trees across the path. As we awkwardly stepped, straddled, climbed, or ducked under each one, trying not to get our packs caught, we stopped counting after fifty. None of these moves felt good to my aching body, protesting as I contorted in irregular ways.

As we settled into a rhythm, laughing occasionally at the awkward positions required, my mind found space to think about Jenni. The urgency to speak up about what I wanted was nagging me.

What do you want?

Crickets—unfortunately, not real ones. I'd spent so long neglecting myself that I no longer knew.

Lather, rinse, repeat.

My thoughts, and my life, had become what felt like an endless, meaningless cycle. As if I were continuously washing my hair, doing nothing to stop the mud from getting right back in it. I was surviving and enduring at work, in my relationship, and in life. It was how I managed to get through each day. I needed to stop hoping for things to get better and start working toward a goal.

I was mercifully saved from another round of repeating thoughts by another body lying on the trail ahead. A man without a race number, looking visibly unhappy. Miles from anywhere, his presence made no sense. He didn't acknowledge us as we passed.

I glanced at Chris. He shrugged, declining to engage or offer help. I wasn't going to interject, I had a race to finish.

Distracted, I almost continued straight on the trail.

Fortunately, Chris said, "Turn left."

A sign with dragons marked the turnoff to Pompey Peak, the final big climb. I was distracted by the man, though I might have missed this sign anyway. I was exhausted and not really seeing what was in front of me. I'd been saved from being lost again. I was certain by this stage in the race the tracking volunteers were being kept extremely busy. I was grateful Chris was here, saving me from another debacle.

Near the summit, we passed a woman coming down with her race bib flapping in the breeze. Hair frazzled, eyes vacant, looking as dirty and destroyed as I felt. We nodded in mutual respect.

At the top, Mount Rainier dominated the northern skyline while Helen appeared impossibly distant to the south. My son and I hugged and took a selfie before enjoying a quiet moment in the sun. I briefly contemplated apologizing for moving so slowly, then stopped myself. I had nothing to be sorry for. This was a great adventure we were able to share, and would never forget.

Returning to the main trail, the man was gone. It was literally all downhill from here, in the good way, with small rolling hills leading to the finish.

I caught a look of pride in my son's eyes as I glanced over. It felt good, though it raised all my internal questions and doubts.

Was I teaching my kids to be the same as me?

No one knew the real me, the vulnerable and most honest parts, because I tried to hide anything that wasn't perfect.

You know they see right through it, just like you did with your mom, don't you?

I was saved from facing this uncomfortable truth as we entered the tree tunnel, exactly as described in the previous finisher's race reports I'd researched online. The path widened to road width, carpeted with bright green grass, and lined by massive, big-leaf maples whose crowns formed a natural roof. These deciduous trees were unusual among the conifers, creating a magical corridor that felt transported from another climate.

Here I entered another time warp. With unchanging scenery, the distance passed slowly. Conversation withered. I'd been tired the first day, exhausted the next two. Now I was simply numb, wanting desperately to run and get this over with, but managing only this determined speed walk.

As boredom, exhaustion, and doubts crept in, I went back to my six steps. It was time for the final step, to visualize the finish. I began imagining what I would do as I crossed the finish line. When I finished my hundred-mile run, I had victoriously put one fist into the air. This time, I decided, I would put up both fists. One for each of the hundred miles I had completed. Jenni, Chris, my mom, and Keith would all be there to cheer me across the finish. I could see it clearly in my mind, and with the vision came belief, purpose, and that little extra energy I needed.

I wondered about how to communicate my victory. Jenni was managing social media posts, so most friends were aware of my status. I considered calling my siblings afterward, though we didn't communicate regularly despite being close. When we did talk, it was as if no time had passed. Yet in any conversation, it was very rare to talk openly about struggles or problems in our lives. When things were good, we had plenty to say. Silence usually indicated problems.

It was especially difficult for any of us to talk about how our upbringing affected us. Nearly impossible to admit that despite Mom's herculean efforts and angelic sacrifices, we'd lacked the consistency of caring parents. We were loved, but not always in the ways we needed.

The experience was different for each of us. For my older brother, Dad was still around, and as firstborn, there was a lot of pressure on him not to disappoint our father. The older middle kids, like me, had some interaction with our dad, who hadn't completely checked out yet. We also experienced Mom's absence as she worked multiple jobs, while going back to school, so she could care for us all. The youngest barely knew their father, but got to live with a mom who had a normal career and time for them. Though they also carried a very different set of expectations and rules. We each carried our scars and challenges, unique to our experiences.

This was not through any fault of our mother, we were all victims of circumstance and necessity. It wouldn't be easy, but if I wanted my life to be different, I had work to do with my family, my kids, and Jenni.

Ahead, I saw someone walking slowly. At first, I thought they might be another runner, then I recognized him as the man who had been lying on the trail ahead of Pompey Peak.

Once we were close enough, he asked, "Is this the right way? To the next place?"

It seemed an odd question. I looked him over, double-checking for a race bib. After determining he wasn't a race participant, I looked for clarification.

"Do you mean Owen's Creek aid station?" I asked.

He nodded.

"Yes, this will get you there," I responded.

"Do you know how far?"

"Somewhere between two and five miles," I answered.

He said nothing, just kept walking slowly.

"Are you out here for the race?" I asked, determining he was not going to offer information.

"I was running with my girlfriend, but she left me behind," he said bitterly.

Ah, that was it. The woman we passed at Pompey Peak. He had been lying on the trail, waiting for her to go up to the top and back, too tired to go with her. It was highly likely he had been holding her back. It was well-known etiquette among runners: if your pacer couldn't keep up, you left them behind.

I cheered her decision mentally. This man's situation highlighted what could have happened with Jeff. I'd lost time going in the wrong direction, but it could have cost me the race if I'd needed to take care of him. She had chosen the other way, and based on what I could see, it was the right decision.

The man was moving slowly, and we quickly left him behind. My thoughts returned to how my lack of vulnerability had affected relationships with my kids. We were very close with one another and loved each other in many ways, but I could now see the wall I'd built between us.

That needs to change. Now.

I could only imagine it came from the exhaustion, that I was too tired to keep walls and defenses up. I was done hiding, and it was time for the truth to come out.

"Hey, Chris."

"Yeah, Dad?"

"I never told you. You remember that long training weekend I had a few weeks back?"

"Over the Fourth of July?"

"Yeah." I took a deep breath. "It went really badly, actually. I pushed too hard, got lost, and things fell apart. So bad, I decided to quit. I wasn't going to do this race because I didn't think I could." I paused to let it sink in for him. "Obviously, I changed my mind and decided to start, but I wasn't sure if I would finish. Not until we started this section."

There. It was out. I was scared. He loved me when I was strong, would he love me now he knew the truth?

"Why didn't you tell me?" he asked.

Fair question.

"Because I was worried you wouldn't believe in me, that you might think I wasn't good enough."

I left the last part hanging, leaving unsaid that it wasn't just the race I wasn't good enough for.

"Dude, are you crazy? I don't care if you did this or not, or if you quit in the middle. I'm proud of you for who you are, not what you do. This is amazing, but it's not why I love you."

I almost cried. Like Joy, he had given me permission to let go of being strong, accepting all of me. Including the imperfect parts.

"I'm going to do better. Reach out more. Tell you all the things in my life, including the ones that aren't so great," I promised.

"Thank you. I'd like that. A lot. Love you, Dad!"

"I love you too!"

We walked in silence as I committed to honesty going forward. Somehow, I'd figure out what I wanted and needed, then ask for it. It would take work, practice, and rough moments, but things would get better.

The tree tunnel gave way to a fire road through pine and fir forest. As if the universe wanted to celebrate, a cart appeared ahead with a bottle of whisky and disposable cups. An unofficial race tradition waiting just before the last aid station. We stopped, and he poured us each a shot.

"Cheers!"

We clinked plastic cups and threw the drinks back. The alcohol hit immediately, unsurprising given my minimal food intake, dehydration, and less than eight hours of sleep in the last four days. The light buzz felt deserved.

Within minutes, I could see the aid station with Jenni waiting, Keith and my mom just behind her. They all looked happy and expectant. Just thirteen more miles to go, yet plenty more work to be done.

It wasn't over yet.

12

Chris and I were almost strutting as we approached Owen's Creek aid station, as much as two thoroughly destroyed humans could manage. Keith waited with a smile, my mother radiating pride beside him. Jenni held another sign she'd smuggled into the Jeep, reading "You're my Superman!" complete with a drawing of the caped hero, fist raised triumphantly.

The image triggered a memory from years ago, a conversation with a friend after a disastrous date where I'd been unable to relax and be myself. I was confident this was yet another first and last date.

"You think you're Clark Kent," my friend said, looking me straight in the eye, "but really you're Superman."

I'd laughed it off, not knowing how to take her assessment.

"You think you're weak and only pretending to be a genuinely good person," she'd continued. "But you have it backwards. Superman acts clumsy as Clark Kent, but really, he's strong. Until you figure out who you really are, you're going to struggle with dating."

I'd deflected and changed the subject then, not thinking of that moment since. Now, in my deep fatigue, I finally heard what she meant.

I was dragged out of my reverie by the noise from Owen's Creek, the final aid station. Mile 193.5, over 95% complete!

An aid station clock displayed it was 7:03 AM Tuesday. When I'd started four days ago, the plan was to finish last night at the latest. Fortunately, even missing that goal by a lot still left ten hours until cutoff, with only thirteen miles ahead.

Anything could happen between here and there, but I'd dealt with the worst the Bigfoot 200 had to offer. Barring catastrophe, I was going to finish.

The energy here was jubilant and contagious, a stark contrast to the zombie-like atmosphere of the last few stations. I found reserves I didn't know existed, grinning stupidly as I stuffed cookies into my mouth. My body craved energy in the quickest form available, and I happily obliged.

I began shedding unnecessary weight. Headlamp, flashlight, extra batteries, protein bars, poncho, gloves, first aid kit, emergency blanket, and water purification straw were yanked out of my bag like an "Everything Must Go" sale. Even my trusty, disgusting bandana, which had served as a sun block, sweat rag, and napkin, was discarded into a bag Jenni held. Anything non-essential was dead weight at this point.

Glancing at the blue sky, I spotted turkey vultures slowly flying overhead, looking for a morsel. "They keep circling," I told an aid station worker, pointing up, "but they won't get me!"

I received a courtesy laugh, more than I deserved. Grabbing a cola for caffeine as much as sugar, I performed a quick mental checklist of anything else I might need before heading out. With the recognition that I was good to go, it suddenly hit me. As someone who had a hard time asking for what I needed, I had been doing a good job.

At first, it hadn't come naturally. I'd had to write up checklists to identify my needs and encourage me to ask for them. Along the course, I'd improved with each station. Here, near the end, I knew instinctively what I required and asked without hesitation. Perhaps, with some practice, I could learn to do the same in my life.

"Do you need anything else?" Jenni asked.

"No, I'm good," I answered, with a quiet laugh to myself at the sincerity of the statement.

"Are you ready?" I asked Jenni with a smile, as she would be pacing me for this last section.

"Absolutely!"

We would travel three miles down this gravel road before completing the last ten miles on streets into the town of Randall, finishing at the high school track. I grabbed Jenni's hand as we started walking. We didn't hold on long, but the moment was nice before our arms decided it was too much extra work.

Ten minutes later, the Jeep rolled past with my crew cheering, hanging out the windows, and waving as they disappeared around a corner. I felt a brief sadness that this would soon end.

Walking in silence, I spent a moment with my mother's parting words at the aid station. She'd grabbed my attention and said very sincerely, "I love you!"

"I love you too, Mom!"

I hadn't thought much of it in the moment, distracted by the activity, but it lingered. For perhaps the first time, I truly heard everything in that declaration. The deep love that had always existed, paired with all her sacrifices over the years. It had always been there.

I'd never doubted her love, though I'd struggled with the loneliness of her absence. I finally saw that both could be true. She could love me unconditionally, and I could still feel alone. I would still have insecurities and anxieties to process, but now I could proceed with the knowledge and confidence that I was truly loved. More importantly, I could accept and trust that love.

You don't call your mom enough.

True. I wanted my kids to reach out more, yet I was equally guilty. I committed to calling more. My mother, kids, and siblings. We all needed to talk more about the things we avoided.

Jenni and I continued in reflective silence through an old-growth forest of Douglas fir and western red cedar, some trees over 400 years old and six feet in diameter. These ancient sentinels had witnessed countless seasons, surviving fires and storms long before Europeans even knew they existed.

The understory here was dominated by sword ferns, their fronds creating a verdant carpet beneath the massive conifers. Occasional patches of devil's club thrust upward with their enormous palmate leaves, while vine maple created a delicate latticework in the filtered sunlight. This was old Cascades forest, the kind that existed when Indigenous peoples roamed these lands, encouraging these giants to thrive.

I regretted not a single moment of this journey. It wasn't over, but even if it ended now, I wouldn't leave empty-handed. I knew I didn't have to be strong anymore, and everyone would be better for it. Clark Kent or Superman, it didn't matter. I was me.

A loud crash accompanied a large black bear, likely a male given the size, bursting from the Douglas firs on our right, sprinting across the road fifty feet in front of us. We froze. The crashing sounds stopped, indicating he'd paused somewhere in the western hemlock grove to our left.

The finish line lay ahead, no way I was turning back. Bears in this area were typically wary of humans, and this one looked as startled as we were. I reached for Jenni's hand, pulling her along as I took a slow step forward.

"Hello, Mr. Bear," I said in a soothing voice.

Silence.

"Just walking by, heading this way. We're cool," I continued as we took another step.

"You do your thing, we'll do ours."

I was answered by a small rustle, revealing him peeking over the salmonberry bushes about a hundred feet away, face turned toward us with apparent curiosity. His relaxed posture suggested no immediate threat. I smiled at him, resisting the urge to wave lest it seem threatening. Jenni remained silent and almost motionless, frightened yet trusting my decision to move forward.

"That's right, we're good. Sorry to disturb you. Have a really good day and stay awesome, okay?" I finished as we eased by.

Once past, I heard branches breaking as he continued his own journey. Jenni silently let out a large breath. It was now clear she had been holding it since Mr. Bear crossed our path. She remained stiff, I knew it would be several minutes before she would completely relax. We picked up the pace, happy to increase distance from both bear and aid station.

That almost gave me a heart attack!

I hadn't worried about my heart once during this entire race, a revelation in itself. Maybe I was releasing that anxiety too. I had a limited number of heartbeats, but instead of counting and worrying each might be the last, I would try to relax and enjoy whatever time remained.

We reached asphalt road and turned left. Real civilization! After days in wilderness, it felt magical, like stepping into sunlight after a matinee show. I found a burst of energy, not enough to run but sufficient for aggressive power-walking. I laughed at the memory of my "sprint" to the finish line of my hundred-miler. Video later revealed it barely qualified as a slow jog.

I stole a glance at Jenni, walking beside me. She had supported me throughout our relationship in many ways. I loved her truly, grateful for everything she brought to my life, yet things needed to change if we were going to move in and build a future together.

Will she still love me when she knows my truth?

I was petrified but knew we were destined for failure if we stayed on this path.

Tell her.

"So, Jenni. You know, while you were in Bali with your friends?"

"Yes," she answered tentatively.

"Well, that training weekend didn't go well..."

I told her everything. The disastrous training days, quitting everything, not leaving bed for more than a day, Joy's intervention, my decision to at least start this race despite thinking I might not finish, and all the shame I'd carried inside the past five weeks.

"I didn't want to tell you because I was afraid you'd think I couldn't do it."

She was silent for a minute as we walked, increasing my anxiety.

"I wish you would have told me," she finally said.

"Me too. I should have, but I was scared. Worried you'd think I wasn't good enough. I dreaded telling you. So, when you got back, and I'd decided to start anyway, I didn't say anything.

"I know it doesn't make it better, but it wasn't just you. I didn't tell anyone.

"I'm sorry, and I'm committed to be more honest about what's happening and how I feel. To you, my kids, my family. Everyone."

"Thank you, and I love you," she replied. "And me too, I'll try to communicate better."

I reached for her hand. She grabbed it and squeezed in love and support. I squeezed back. We released and walked on in comfortable silence.

I'd built enormous anxiety around this moment. I had been so hard on myself for that weekend's failure. In the end, the people closest to me didn't care how far I ran or how strong I appeared. They just wanted me to be happy. I'd been running to find worthiness and love when I'd had it all along.

I was running to prove to others that I was strong and capable. I'd been fooling myself if I thought they didn't see the truth, no matter how deep I buried it. The same way I saw it in my mom, they all saw right through me.

We came upon another runner limping between his pacers, leaning hard to the left, his body finished but marching on anyway. We offered words of encouragement as we passed.

As we left them behind, Jenni spoke, a slight hint of defensiveness in her voice. "You know I didn't understand why you wanted to do this. It made no sense to me. I supported you, but I was against it."

"Yes," I acknowledged.

"Well, I get it now. I finally understand why you do these things. I want you to know I support you unconditionally, and if you want to do anything like this again, I'm there."

I was speechless. If I weren't dehydrated, paired with a lifetime's experience suppressing tears, I might have cried. It felt extraordinary to finally be seen. She couldn't possibly understand everything, but she could see the struggle and overcoming I experienced out here. The adventure we were sharing enabled her to understand this part of me I'd been unable to explain.

"Thank you," I mumbled.

My instinct took over immediately, filling this beautiful moment with doubt and delivering a memory from when I won my weight class in the junior high wrestling championship. My father, who normally paid me little attention, insisted I wear my medal while he paraded me around his friends. It felt good, but didn't last. I was only good enough when winning big, and even then, only long enough for the victory lap.

Just one of a multitude of examples of my father's legitimate neglect, minus any halo of love, excepted only upon the rarity I had something that benefited him. Another gift full of anxieties I would need to sort through, though, like his presence, these wounds felt distant.

I worried this might be similar with Jenni, that she was seeing me only in this brief moment. I wanted lasting change, to be seen as myself.

As we entered town, the sparse farms we'd passed gave way to buildings, and there were now cars on the roads. There was not far left to go now, but the work wasn't done.

"Hey. Can we agree to do things differently?" I blurted out.

"What do you mean?"

"I've promised to be more open, to share when I'm scared or stressed or have bad training days and decide to quit."

"Yes," she agreed.

"Well, I need to tell you everything. Including when my feelings are hurt. Or when I'm unhappy."

"Are you unhappy?" She sounded surprised.

"No! Well... yes. Maybe?" I hesitated. "I don't know what I am, to be honest. I've spent so much time trying to be what I think everyone wants me to be, trying to be strong and take care of others.

"I think I'm happy. Pretty sure, anyway. But I don't know for certain. I need some time to figure out what I want, and how to make it real."

Jenni looked concerned, perhaps afraid.

"I want you to be happy," she said sincerely, shadowed with worry.

"To be clear, I want to be happy with you. Figure this out together, be a team again. Like here, where we did it so well. And I need to think about myself and figure out what I really want."

"It's a deal. I'm with you," she agreed, her confidence returning.

"One more thing." I summoned courage to continue. "I'm not sure I'm ready to move in with you until we figure this out. I'm scared otherwise things won't go well, and I don't want us to fall apart."

There. I'd said it. The words I'd been terrified to speak for months, afraid even to admit to myself. I feared that saying I wasn't ready would make her leave, but now I knew moving in before fixing our dynamic would certainly be the end.

"I get it. That makes sense," she finally said after a hesitant pause. "I wish it was different, but I want things to work too. If this is what you need, that's what we'll do."

It felt like another half-concession, as if she were appeasing me rather than offering unconditional support, but it was enough for now. I'd turned her attitude about this race around, I could win her over here too.

We reached the other side of town, turning right onto a long, straight back road leading to the high school. The last mile. I felt tears wanting release, suppressing them with mastery.

I'd spent a lifetime holding emotions back. They got in the way, caused worry, didn't make me feel good. Rather than suffer pain, I'd learned to bury feelings deep in the moment, later rationalizing them, alone, into something manageable. This way, I appeared strong, my feelings didn't bother anyone, and I survived.

I endured.

What if I let my feelings out?

I answered myself immediately, without even a second's pause.

That would be wrong.

The response was so instinctual, I almost didn't hear it. In my head, I was automatically labeling feelings right and wrong. Joy and happiness were acceptable, within reason. Fear and anger were not. There wasn't a place for "wrong" feelings in my life, so I held onto them.

Let them go.

This quiet voice gave the permission I'd longed for. With this freedom, emotions erupted like Mount Saint Helens, decades of pressure finally releasing. Joy for half a second, then sadness, laughter, anger, fear. Each emotion passed through me briefly before the next poured out. A tear ran down my cheek.

I felt lighter and slowly began running with strength I'd thought long gone. Another tear fell, and then I was crying as they poured out. Jenni glanced over and saw the tears, but I didn't care. She started crying too.

I felt everything, and it was good. Even pain felt right and healing. Relief washed over me as I recognized that whatever I was feeling was okay. Scared was all right. Anger was valid. Sadness was legitimate. With each of these "wrong" feelings, I knew happiness deeper, fuller. Joy felt bigger.

Like Helen, I had erupted. There was a lifetime of pressure to release. This wasn't the end, but definitely a beginning. I would never be the same. Time to let go of everything I'd been carrying and give it over to the fire. Like the blast zone I'd traversed, there would be scars on my soul, but like her, I would carry on.

I looked to Jenni, and we smiled at each other with ear-to-ear grins. I looked up at the sky, soaking up sun. Returning my gaze to the road, the school came into view with Chris, Keith, and my mother waiting by the gate.

We turned right into the parking lot, and nothing hurt anymore. I felt pure ecstasy. The clock no longer mattered as I paused to hug everyone. We walked through the gate together into the football stadium. The final quarter-mile around the track lay ahead, the finish line visible. A final, cruel joke from Candice, the race director, required us to go around the track to reach the inflated blue arch.

Choosing to see it as a victory lap, I pulled off my pack and handed it to Jenni, looking deep into her tear-wet eyes. Keith grinned at me, having stayed long after his pacing obligation ended. My mother radiated unconditional love. Chris beamed with pride. I thought of Joy across the state at work, who'd kept me on course when I needed it most.

"35!"

Dave ran over, looking as tired as any runner. He'd been working hard, as had all volunteers, to make this possible. We hugged tightly. We were strangers, yet he had been instrumental in my success, and I was grateful for him and all the others who had given of themselves for us.

"Congratulations, man. Go get it!"

I stepped onto the track for my final quarter-mile. I should have run, but instead I walked, soaking in the moment. I didn't want to forget this. Late morning sun peeking above western red cedars, blue sky peppered with a few small clouds, leaves dancing in a light breeze as a red-tailed hawk circled overhead. In the distance, the Cascade Mountains, where I'd spent these days, stretched through Oregon toward Mount Shasta in California, their volcanic peaks built from millions of years of tectonic collision and magmatic intrusion.

Flags along the stands represented the many countries runners had traveled from to participate in this journey through some of the most pristine rainforest remaining in North America.

I'd started this race trying to prove I was strong. Along the way, I'd discovered I was so much more. This had forever changed me, there was no going back from what I'd learned on these trails through old-growth forests that somehow fed me their wisdom gained over the centuries.

It was time to stop running away from fears and anxieties and start running toward something better. Maybe 200 miles was the distance. I'd proven I was good enough and, more importantly, accepted who I was.

Coming around the last bend into the final hundred

yards, I started running as fast as these demolished legs could go. These final steps were among the easiest of the race, despite exhaustion. Passing under the arch, I held up both hands in victory.

Over 100 hours to finish. Four days and nights in the Cascade Mountains, through ecosystems that ranged from volcanic moonscapes to cathedral forests, into valleys carved by ancient rivers, and over peaks built by millions of years of geological patience.

I was finally able to stop.

13

I wandered around the finish line like a tourist without a map, unsure what came next. Everything for nine months had been about reaching this moment, I'd never really considered what lay beyond. My crew, nearly as exhausted as I was, drifted with me in a zombie-like procession.

Is it really over?

I'd crossed the finish line, yet completion felt oddly elusive.

The food table held no appeal, despite my not eating properly in days. After staring at options with blank eyes, I moved on to the table with finisher belt buckles, each handmade by a local artisan. I selected my favorite, knowing it would occupy a place of honor at home.

I sat in a nearby chair, thinking it would feel wonderful, but couldn't remain still. Four days of desperately wanting rest, and now my body refused to stop. Everything felt anticlimactic. I'd finished, had my brief celebration, and now... nothing. Not that I had energy for festivities, but it seemed oddly quiet for such an accomplishment.

My delayed finish meant Chris and my mother had missed their originally booked flights. Even with last-minute changes, they needed to leave immediately for the airport. At Chris's rental car, we hugged tightly.

"I got you something," he said, reaching into his pocket to produce a trail-marking dragon. "Thought you'd want one, you've been following them for days."

"Where did you get it?" My first concern was whether he'd taken it from the course, potentially leaving runners behind me lost.

"They had a pile over there." He indicated the finish line. "I asked, and they said I could take one."

My worry alleviated, I gave an enthusiastic "Thank you!"

I'd expected never wanting to see another dragon, but instead it felt like an old friend. These orange and pink ribbons tied to clothespins had guided me through this adventure, leading the way forward during hot days and dark nights, assuring me I wasn't lost. It would hang somewhere in my home as evidence that part of being strong meant admitting when I wasn't. That there was more strength in vulnerability than in pretending to be something I wasn't.

Each time I saw it, I'd do an internal check to ensure I was honoring the commitments made in these mountains, that I wasn't straying from the path.

After sending Chris off, I crawled into the Jeep's backseat with blanket and pillow, assuming I'd sleep immediately on the two-hour drive home. Instead, my body couldn't find comfort, and my mind wouldn't shut down. I kept tossing and turning without rest.

"Anyone hungry?" Keith asked.

"Yes," Jenni responded right away.

I still wasn't hungry, but they needed to eat, and it was my turn to take care of them. Thirty minutes later, in a booth at a roadside restaurant, I stared at a menu where nothing appealed despite days without proper meals. After long races, it often took a day or more for my hunger to return, but this hadn't been a normal race and I imagined I'd be starving.

"He just ran 200 miles," Keith announced proudly to our server when she arrived.

She looked confused before offering an obligatory "Wow."

It struck me that while I'd spent a hundred hours in the wilderness pushing my limits, the world had gone about its business without notice. Our server was evidence it neither knew nor cared. That was fine, this one had been for me.

We sat in burned-out silence waiting for food. When it arrived, I managed less than half of my cheeseburger. It tasted flat, making my stomach churn. I'd thought this first meal would taste amazing, but it didn't. It had nothing to do with the chef, my body didn't have energy left for taste buds. Or digesting. Or really anything, apparently, including sleep.

"You know what," I said, turning to Jenni with a smile, "while out there I had a lot of time to think, and I came to one serious conclusion."

"What's that?"

"I want you to know I love you. Very much. However, after this race, I can say with confidence that I would not walk 500 miles, and definitely would not walk 500 more, just to be at your door," I responded with a playful grin, referring to the Proclaimers' song.

Jenni laughed as Keith chuckled, our first levity in days. We all loosened up, though conversation remained sparse as we finished and loaded back into the car. I still couldn't sleep as the last of the drive passed.

At home, I groaned as I extracted myself like a contortionist from the Jeep, though much less graceful. During the drive, my muscles had stiffened and locked, making movement difficult and painful. Keith hugged us goodbye and headed back to his life while Jenni and I took one look at the Jeep's chaotic contents and closed the door. Future problems for future selves.

Inside, I let Jenni shower first. In addition to being chivalrous, I needed the extra time. Just removing my shoes seemed herculean. Struggling to pull my shirt off over my head, I was surprised that my arms were as useless as everything else.

When the shirt finally released, I caught a whiff that was thoroughly unpleasant.

The poor people in the restaurant!

It was the same when I peeled off my socks. The shower was stopping just as I managed to pull my shorts free, to another wave of stink.

I stared down at legs literally caked in mud and blood where they'd been exposed, while areas covered by socks and shorts were merely dirty.

Why does anybody do this?

I had zero regrets.

The hot shower felt amazing initially as I watched dirt swirl down the drain with detached enjoyment.

Ouch!

I was discovering exactly where there was chafing. The water burned and stung where skin had been rubbed raw, continuing to ache even after the water had moved on.

Everything was now flaring up with pain. Reaching for soap hurt. I could barely reach down to wash my legs and feet or bring my arms up to wash my hair. The soap burned the raw skin even more. Normally, a shower after a long run was heaven, today, not so much. I kept showering because I wanted to get as much dirt, grime, and smell off me as possible before I climbed into the waiting bed.

The heat loosened my muscles, and I began to feel truly sleepy. After the awkward step out of the shower and drying off, I struggled into comfy, warm pajamas. My last task done, I stumbled to bed where Jenni was already asleep. I was out before my head hit the pillow.

Sixteen hours later, the alarm cut through the exercise-induced coma.

Why is the stupid thing going off?

As Jenni stirred, I remembered. She was flying out for a work event she couldn't miss. Bad timing, but unavoidable.

I was going to have to move too, I was her ride to the airport.

Getting up was a slog. Every muscle ached, even ones I didn't know existed. I was still exhausted and hurt everywhere.

Worth it.

I'd proven I was strong enough and learned I didn't need to be.

Glancing at Jenni pulling on clothes, I could name a thousand reasons I loved her. My relationship struggles had never been because she was evil or bad, but rather because I hadn't spoken up about my needs while trying to be strong. Never revealing I wanted to be loved and cared for. I didn't speak my truths and conceded to her. Then I resented her for it. I carried blame for how things were. Changing the future was up to me.

Starting to stand, I immediately fell back to the bed.

"Are you okay?" Jenni asked, concerned.

"Can't stand up," I eked out after a second failed attempt.

"Your legs?"

"No. My feet. Feels like stepping on Legos."

I searched the floor for whatever was causing grief. Nothing but carpet. Lifting my feet revealed layers of medical tape with wrinkled white skin squeezing out between, still looking corpse-like. Nothing should have given the sensation of stepping on tiny, sharp rocks.

I tried again. Pain.

Staring again at the beaten mush that was now my feet, it became clear. They'd been macerated by pounding, rocky terrain, and constant wetness. I cursed the waterproof shoes. Thousands of micro-tears in muscles and mini-fractures in bones.

"I'll be okay, I just utterly abused my feet," I told Jenni, forcing myself up.

Every step felt like walking on jagged pebbles as I limped to find my bougiest slippers. They helped, but every step still sent a pang of discomfort ricocheting around my limbs.

The rest of me felt surprisingly good. Tired and achy, but more like after a long training weekend than four days of torture. Emitting small "ows" with each step made the situation slightly funny, lightening both my pain and my mood.

We loaded her suitcase on top of the mess in the back of the Jeep and started the drive. I decided to use the opportunity to practice asking for what I needed, dropping her at the terminal curb rather than walking her to security like I usually would. She was all in.

"Thank you. So much. I don't know if I could have done it without you," I said sincerely.

"You were amazing! I was happy to be out there with you," she replied with tears in her eyes.

"When you get back, we'll celebrate and talk about us, our future, what it could look like."

We hugged, holding each other for a long time. After a kiss, she walked away. I watched until she disappeared into the building before walking around to the driver's side with quiet "ows" to myself accompanying each step.

EPILOGUE

This trail I was running on was an old, familiar friend. I'd run it countless times, training for Bigfoot 200 and many more since. It comforted me. Not difficult, every twist and turn known like the back of my hand, allowing me to relax and run on autopilot. Perfect for lazy Saturday mornings like today.

It was almost exactly six months since the finish line, a good reason to get out and run. I eased up the short hill starting the trail, a nice way to jump-start the heart. I wouldn't push hard today, but it took time for my body to settle and find rhythm. A good push at the beginning helped.

Over the top and onto easy, slow rollers, my breathing eased. Lately, I'd been running faster yet with less effort, perhaps because I no longer felt chased. No anxiety or fear along for the ride. I was here because I wanted to be, and not to escape. There was nothing left to run from in the moment. Such an amazing feeling, running for pleasure, simply because I wanted to.

I had worried that after Bigfoot 200 I wouldn't want to run anymore, that I'd burn myself out, but it was better than ever. Of course, I didn't start immediately—it took weeks for my feet to heal, over a month for muscle aches to fade, and a couple months for mental grogginess to clear completely.

My first run came a few weeks after the race, slow and steady, yet full of energy, engine ready to go. That's when I first felt freedom from the chase and knew I'd keep running, only now for me. No need to prove anything anymore.

I still carried a feeling of accomplishment, but it never became what I expected. I'd anticipated every moment a celebration, feeling free and happy with rainbows and unicorns for a long time thereafter. Instead of unbridled joy, there was simply a general sense of contentment.

The race transformed me, but the world didn't change.

Approaching the next hill, bigger than the first, I took a deep breath. I liked this run's front-loaded work in exchange for downhills and flats on the return. While I enjoyed finishing strong during training, today called for floating through to the end. I needed it, last night had been tough for sleep.

I wanted to blame disrupted sleeping patterns on the race, making it difficult to return to regular schedules. That may have been true the first few months, but lately, sleepless nights were because of Jenni.

Things started well when she returned from her work trip, both still riding the high from the race. Yet as I practiced asking for what I wanted and needed, we struggled. As I changed, she fought to stay the same. When I suggested counseling, she refused.

Three short months from discussing moving in together to breaking up.

The separation was initially devastating. I started regressing into depression, but I'd learned to talk about feelings with family and friends. They helped me regain perspective. We hadn't broken up because I wasn't enough, but because sometimes things change.

I felt gratitude not because it ended, but for how much I'd gained along the way. We'd been great together in our time. Parts of me wished things had turned out differently, but I wouldn't be where I was without the path traveled. All the good and bad helped me finally discover who I was and what I wanted. It was sadly for the best.

Barking ahead brought me back to the trail. Cindy and John approached with their dog, Buddy. We'd become acquainted through frequent trail encounters, and I was always happy to greet him. He ran up as I leaned down for love, tail wagging. After quick hellos, we continued our separate ways.

I was grateful for the interlude, having hoped today's run would carry less sadness. I was slowly healing, one day at a time. On the positive side, things had improved in the rest of my life. Relationships with my mother, siblings, and children had all gotten better.

I am loved.

The thought came with warmth. I knew it as fact. The trick was to remember.

Seeing my mother at the race helped differentiate the years she sacrificed everything to raise us versus the years since we became adults, finally relieving her burden. She'd always loved us very much. I was thankful that now she could be here when needed, supporting me in person as she had always done in spirit. She did the best she could with what she had, and it had always been enough. Though if she was anything like me, it never felt that way.

I am enough.

She wasn't a perfect parent, but neither was I.

Is anyone?

All parents struggle through mistakes. In that space, we'd both done our best with the available tools. I could only hope I'd given my kids enough to do things better than I had.

My relationships with Chris and Joy improved dramatically through openness, though I couldn't undo historical damage. At least I'd broken current patterns, giving them chances to see they could do things differently too. We couldn't change the past, but we could affect the future.

It felt good knowing my kids saw the real me. The dad who worked hard, did his best, made mistakes, and was more than enough. To them, I was a good father, and they loved me not because I was strong and flawless, but because I was imperfectly me. The same way I loved my mother and siblings. The same way they loved me back.

Emerging from Douglas fir and western hemlock forest into a clearing, I could see Mount Hood clearly, its sharp, snow-capped point piercing sky, like a granite spear thrust upward by millennia of tectonic collision, one reason I loved this run. To the left, Mount Adams' rounded top rose white and glistening, its volcanic bulk testament to the Cascade Range's geological drama. On the far left, I could make out Mount Saint Helens, Helen to me, her jagged crater reflecting sun, forever changed by the eruption that had created the blast zone I'd traversed.

Each mountain told stories of Earth's restless energy. Andesite and dacite flows, pyroclastic deposits, glacial carving, and retreat. The very ground beneath my feet was built from their ancient eruptions, rich volcanic soils supporting the temperate rainforest ecosystem I'd been running through.

After the break-up, my mother had mailed me a quote from author Brianna Wiest, which I taped to my computer monitor. "One day, the mountain that is in front of you will be so far behind you it will barely be visible in the distance. But the person you become in learning to get over it? That will stay with you forever. And that is the point of the mountain."

It couldn't have been more accurate. I took a deep breath and soaked in the good moment, a rarity these days. I wanted to make it last.

Turning back toward my car, it felt good to be a runner.

Yes, I am a runner.

I'd finally accepted this truth. Not professional or skilled, but indeed a runner. The realization brought memories of Coach Craig, who'd gifted so much with his advice over the years. Another of his talks came to mind while we were gathered before the morning's bike ride.

"How many of you can sing?" he asked.

Four out of fifty raised hands.

"How many are artists?"

A few more hands.

"Dancers?"

A few for that too.

"If I ask these questions of five-year-olds," he said, "every hand goes up. Every one of them can sing, paint, and dance.

"As we grow older, we judge and compare ourselves. If we can't sing quite as well as someone else, suddenly we believe we can't sing. Or draw. Or dance. We think because we're not as good as someone else, we can't do it. The truth is, you can do all those things and more.

"You don't have to be good at it to do what you love. Be like a child, and don't let anything stop you."

They were wise words I was still digesting years later. I had finally accepted I was a runner. And worthy and loved. Also, not perfect. The beautiful thing was both could be true. I was imperfectly perfect. Or perfectly imperfect.

More mountains lay ahead, more challenges to face. I could sense a bigger peak looming on the horizon, but this one was behind me.

Hitting the last two miles, I felt good. I appreciated all the good things that brought me here and felt optimistic about the future. The road ahead would be difficult, but I could do it. I'd started Bigfoot 200 hoping it would be the distance that fixed everything. Turned out it wasn't the right distance for everything, but it was the right distance for me.

Not because I was strong enough, but because I finally realized I didn't have to be strong to do hard things.

SIX STEPS TO COMPLETING YOUR 1,000 MILE JOURNEY

The Chinese philosopher Lao Tzu said, "The journey of a thousand miles begins with a single step." Here are the six steps I created to get myself across the finish line of the Bigfoot 200. For more on these, and how they can help you complete whatever long journey awaits you, visit: www.hardthingsbook.com

1. **Take the First Step** – Whatever your challenge, start.
2. **Stay Healthy** – Take care of you.
3. **Have Fun** – Enjoy the ride!
4. **Take It In Segments** – Focus on what's in front of you.
5. **Adapt** – Flow like a river.
6. **Visualize the Finish** – Believe you will.

ACKNOWLEDGMENTS

A huge Thank You to Shana, this book would not be what it is without you. I appreciate you and your infinite wisdom and patience.

A very big Thank You to Cami Ostman at The Narrative Project, and Jessica Carew Kraft, writer and editor extraordinaire.

Many Thanks for all the help, time, and input from Jennifer, Jeanne, Vince, Melody, Maria, and all the amazing people at Atmosphere Press who turned my simple document into a beautiful book.

Thank you for being part of the journey in one or more of many different forms to Katie, Anna, Larry, Ching, Mark, Richard, Candice and Destination Trail Races, the Volunteers at the 2017 Bigfoot 200 and trail events everywhere, and hosts Don & Scott of the Trail Runner Nation Podcast.

Thank you for all the love and continuing memories to my Mom and family—Michael, Lexi, Gray, Kathy, Sean, Mike, Jon, Ben, Shannon, and Ari—plus all the many spouses, in-laws, nieces, nephews, aunts, uncles, cousins, and more that make up our large and amazing family. Love you all!

ABOUT ATMOSPHERE PRESS

Founded in 2015, Atmosphere Press was built on the principles of Honesty, Transparency, Professionalism, Kindness, and Making Your Book Awesome. As an ethical and author-friendly hybrid press, we stay true to that founding mission today.

If you're a reader, enter our giveaway for a free book here:

SCAN TO ENTER
BOOK GIVEAWAY

If you're a writer, submit your manuscript for consideration here:

SCAN TO SUBMIT
MANUSCRIPT

And always feel free to visit Atmosphere Press and our authors online at atmospherepress.com. See you there soon!

ABOUT THE AUTHOR

Marc Hopkins is an endurance athlete, author, and speaker who has completed the Bigfoot 200, eight Iron-distance triathlons, and more than 200 events ranging from 5Ks to triathlons to ultramarathons. He holds an Executive MBA and has coached hundreds of athletes across their own finish lines—including the mental barriers that matter as much as the physical ones. Marc lives in the Portland, Oregon area, where he spends his time exploring the trails of the Pacific Northwest and the deeper questions that endurance reveals, including family, love, and the reasons we keep running.

www.ingramcontent.com/pod-product-compliance
Ingram Content Group UK Ltd.
Pitfield, Milton Keynes, MK11 3LW, UK
UKHW042000080626
12989UKWH00003B/181

9 798901 742426